Grade Your Child's School

BY CHARLES HARRISON

CAREER PRESS
180 FIFTH AVENUE
P.O. BOX 34
HAWTHORNE, NJ 07507
1-800-CAREER-1
201-427-0229 (OUTSIDE U.S.)
FAX: 201-427-2037

Grade Your Child's School
ISBN 1-56414-127-6, $14.99
Cover design by The Visual Group
Printed in the U.S.A. by Book-mart Press

To order this title by mail, please include price as noted above, $2.50 handling per order, and $1.00 for each book ordered. Send to: Career Press, Inc., 180 Fifth Ave., P.O. Box 34, Hawthorne, NJ 07507

Or call toll-free 1-800-CAREER-1 (Canada: 201-427-0229) to order using VISA or MasterCard, or for further information on books from Career Press.

Library of Congress Cataloging-in-Publication Data

Harrison, Charles Hampton, 1932–
    Grade your child's school / by Charles Harrison.
        p.   cm.
    Includes bibliographical references and index.
    ISBN 1-66414-127-6 (paper) : $14.99
    1. Schools--United States--Evaluation.   2. Education--United States--Evaluation.   3. School choice--United States.   I. Title.
LA210.H38   1995
371'.00973--dc20   95-4012
                                                                          CIP

T A B L E   O F   C O N T E N T S

PART 1

Introduction:
Why This Book Is Needed

This book has become necessary because of three trends in America today: (1) the population is increasingly mobile, (2) more states and school districts are offering parents real choice in school selection, and (3) parents generally take a more active role in trying to match their child with the "right" educational program and the "right" physical and social environment.

The federal government conservatively estimates that a million or more families are on the move every year. They may be leaving a city for suburbia or a rural community, or vice versa; they may be going no farther than the next county; or they may be heading for the opposite coast.

In 1988, I wrote a book called *Public Schools USA* (a second edition was published in 1991). The book provided statistical data for hundreds of public school districts in major metropolitan areas. That was a good first step toward helping parents. This book is the crucial second step. Now, parents themselves are able to evaluate any individual school—public, private, or parochial—anywhere in the country.

I was reminded again while collecting information for *Public Schools USA* that, even in those public school districts whose statistics make them look very good on paper, the quality of education and the physical plant can vary considerably among schools in a district. It was not uncommon, for example, that someone in a district would warn that the schools on one side of town had better teachers and more up-to-date teaching or learning materials than schools across the tracks or highway. Therefore, a family might select a particular public school district in which to move, but still want to evaluate two or three schools in that district before deciding where to send their child, or, for that matter, what neighborhood to move into.

Another family might wish to consider several private and parochial schools in a given area where they plan to relocate. Again, each school, including those in a single parish or diocese, might differ significantly from every other school. "Private schools have been stereotyped as being all of one kind," says Catherine O'Neill of the National Association of Independent Schools (NAIS), "but that simply is not true. There is wide variety in student bodies, missions, and education philosophies. Some schools have a very loose teaching/learning environment, for example, while others are very structured."

Some support exists for at least allowing parents to choose any public school for their child, although parents may then be responsible for transportation beyond the district or neighborhood where they live. In other words, the time may soon be at hand when no family has to be content with sending their child to the school in their neighborhood or even a school in their district, municipality, or county. Already, in Ohio and Washington and in public school districts scattered throughout the country, parents can choose to send their child to any school in their home district. In Arkansas, Idaho, Iowa, Minnesota, Nebraska, and Utah, parents may send their child to a school outside their home district without paying tuition, although they may have to provide their own transportation.

In such large urban districts as Dade County, Florida (includes Miami); Kansas City, Missouri; and Richmond, California; and in some small districts such as Montclair, New Jersey, parents already exercise school choice within their district. They are able to choose from among many so-called magnet schools (see Part 2, Glossary of Terms). In those districts, the only factors affecting parental choice are available space (some schools, naturally, are more popular than others) and desegregation policy. Some districts operate under a desegregation plan that requires racial balance in all schools.

In his 1994 State of the Union address, President Clinton advocated more charter schools, which are public schools that operate in a manner similar to private schools (see glossary). Also, for a number of years, many politicians and some educators have called for a voucher system that would allow parents to choose from among public, private, and parochial schools (see glossary).

Finally, this book is needed because more and more parents are willing and able to voice their demands for better education and improved physical plant. Almost gone are the days when parents, like their children in the classrooms, were to be seen but not heard. Increasingly, parents want to examine carefully the educational program in a school before sending their children there. Where school-based management is practiced (throughout Kentucky, for example), parents are even working side by side with teachers and administrators to shape the educational program. Parents are ready, then, to ask tough questions, to make careful observations, and to be thorough in their collection of information.

The education editor for a major national newspaper once told me that when he visited a school, his first stop was always the boys' lavatory, not because he had to go there but because of what it told him about the school. If the lavatory was in need of immediate attention, he said, it was likely that the educational program was also.

Of course, there is more to evaluating a school than simply peeking in rest rooms. A fair and thorough evaluation requires making more than one observation, asking a number of pointed questions, and collecting pertinent data. That is what this book is all about: What should parents look for as they decide where to enroll their child?

The book is divided into two major divisions. One division (Part 3) is devoted to evaluating an elementary school; the other division (Part 4) focuses on the secondary school. Each of these two parts includes five sections: (1) what parents should know about their child, (2) questions to ask, (3) observations to make, (4) data to collect, and (5) workbook pages to write in answers and notes.

Where did the suggested questions and observations come from? Who decided what information parents need in order to make the best decision for their child's education? You can thank hundreds of people: parents and principals of public and private schools scattered throughout the country who were interviewed in person or by telephone, nearly 700 men and women who responded to a survey of elementary school principals conducted in cooperation with the National Association of Elementary School Principals, and staff personnel of major national education organizations. (See Appendix A for a more complete explanation of how the guidebook was developed.)

To the best of my knowledge, this is the first time that such large numbers of educators and laypersons throughout America have reached consensus on what criteria parents should use when evaluating a school. Parents who use this book wisely to make wise decisions may affect not only the education of their own child but perhaps even the future direction of education in the United States.

PART 2

What Are They Talking About? A Glossary of Terms

E veryone uses jargon and technical terms sometimes, words and phrases that are peculiar to his or her profession or job. Printers work with fonts and picas; pilots may measure the speed of their aircraft at Mach 1 or Mach 2; and hospital staffs respond to calls of stat and code blue.

School administrators and teachers have their own jargon and technical terms, and they use them frequently. To make matters worse, they don't always explain to parents and other laypersons what the terms mean. For example, if the school reports that results of the grade-equivalency test in reading show that your third-grader is reading at a sixth-grade level, does that really mean he or she is capable of reading sixth-grade materials? (The answer is No.)

Speaking of tests, do the terms *authentic assessment* and *standardized testing* mean the same thing? Do you want your child engaged in *cooperative learning*? And, by the way, what exactly is an *alternative school*?

This part of the guidebook offers a glossary of educators' jargon and technical terms. The glossary should help you frame your questions for principals and teachers. Even more importantly, it should help you understand the answers.

The jargon and explanations are organized under some of the same categories used later for your suggested questions. For example, grade-equivalency and authentic assessment are found under the Testing heading; cooperative learning is listed in the Teachers category; and the alternative school is defined under Administration/Organization. The categories are arranged alphabetically, as is the jargon in each category.

Good hunting (meaning "to search" or "to seek").

ADMINISTRATION/ORGANIZATION

Ability grouping: Assigning students to courses and classrooms according to their perceived ability and actual achievement.

For example, students taking algebra may be assigned to a particular level of algebra (from most demanding to least demanding) and to particular teachers and classrooms according to their achievement in other math courses and on the basis of recommendations made by previous teachers or counselors. (See also Tracking.)

Alternative school: A school that may be designed for gifted students or those with learning problems. But more often than not, an alternative school is for students who are incorrigible or have been frequently disciplined for disrupting regular classes.

Blue-ribbon school: Used to denote an elementary or secondary school that has been recognized by the federal or state government, or both, for educational excellence. The award is based on such criteria as demonstrated leadership, student achievement tests scores, attendance records, number of high school graduates going on to higher education, and honors received by a school's teachers and students.

Carnegie unit: One Carnegie unit equals 120 hours spent on one subject during the year (for example, five 40-minute periods per week for 36 weeks). A high school may require a student to complete a certain number of Carnegie units in English, mathematics, science, etc., in order to graduate.

Chapter 1: A federally funded program that offers remedial (catch-up) instruction for students in elementary grades.

Charter school: Also referred to as a contract school, it allows a group of teachers, parents, and other citizens to organize and run a school that is not controlled by a public board of education but is accountable to that board and supported by public funds.

Comprehensive school: A secondary school that offers under one roof usually three courses of study: college preparatory, vocational, and general studies.

Demographics: The collection and study of statistics about a population; for example: age, sex, race, ethnic and cultural backgrounds, and family income.

Head start: A successful federally funded program to help children aged 3 and 4, usually from low-income families, to get ready for school.

Magnet school: An elementary or secondary (middle/high) school that specializes in a specific subject area (for example, the arts, communication, science) or a particular approach to learning (for example, highly structured or cooperative learning). All magnet schools in a district generally provide the same basic curriculum.

Mainstreaming: More and more districts are including students with physical handicaps and minor emotional/mental handicaps in regular classrooms as often as possible, rather than placing them in separate classrooms. The practice also is called *inclusion.*

Montessori: An educational system named for Dr. Maria Montessori that emphasizes structured, hands-on learning, but flexible grouping, which allows children to progress according to their individual development rather than their age or grade.

Open education: Opposite of self-contained classroom. A number of students, perhaps equivalent to several classes, is organized in a large, open space. This may be called *multi-age* grouping. The open space may be subdivided into small work areas by shelving or other nonpermanent and low partitions. Students often move from one study group to another at the direction of one of several teachers who work with and guide the study groups but seldom lecture to the entire body.

Outcome-based education: A new term for what schools were always presumed to be doing: determining what skills and knowledge students are supposed to possess at the end of a course or period of instruction (learning outcomes) and holding students and their teachers responsible for achieving those goals.

Pull-out: A program whereby students identified as being gifted and those with mental, emotional, or physical handicaps are separated from regular classes for part or all of the school day for special instruction.

Restructuring: A general overhaul of a single school or an entire district. Some of the key elements are as follows: greater emphasis on varied approaches to student learning (e.g., students working mostly in small groups) and less on traditional teaching methods (e.g., lecturing to students sitting in straight rows), evaluating students on the basis of their performance rather than their answers on standardized tests (see Testing: *authentic assessment*), and more involvement of students' parents and the community at large in curriculum and other policy decisions (see *School-based management*).

School-based management: Major school decisions are made jointly by the principal, designated teachers and parents, and— in some cases— older students. As a team, they draft education goals and a spending plan for their school based on the general requirements of a higher authority (usually a board of trustees). This means that the team may make some curriculum decisions and decide priorities for their school's budget and how to spend funds provided by the higher authority. (*Note:* the system sometimes is referred to as *site-based management.*)

Self-contained classroom: Where a group of students of approximately the same age and grade spend most of the school day together in one room and usually with a single teacher.

Tracking: Based on their achievement, aptitude, and future goals, students are placed usually in one of three tracks: college preparatory, vocational/technical and general studies. (See also Administration/Organization: *ability grouping* and *comprehensive school.*)

Voucher system: A plan whereby parents would receive a voucher worth a certain amount of money (based on the average current expense per pupil in the state or area). The parents could then choose whether to spend that money in a public, private, or parochial school.

CURRICULUM

Advanced placement: A program sponsored by the College Board that enables above-average high school students to study a number of subjects at a college (advanced) level and then take exams that may assure them of college credit for their work.

Affective education: Refers to lessons or projects that help students relate basic subject matter to their own lives and their place in society. For example, students learning about the history of racism in a social studies course might act out an encounter between students of different races and cultures and then discuss their reactions to the role playing.

Basal reader: A book used in the primary grades to help children learn to read simple words and stories.

Bilingual education: A program whereby students whose native language is not English receive basic instruction in their native language while learning to read and write English. Schools may vary in the amount of instruction conducted in the native language. (See also Curriculum: *ESL.*)

CD-ROM: Computer discs that may include a wide variety of information, including encyclopedias and indexes to additional sources. The Encyclopaedia Britannica, for example, is now available on CD-ROM.

Computer literacy: Knowledge of how a computer operates and how to use one.

Creationism: Science instruction in some private and public schools includes the Old Testament version of the world's creation by God. The biblical version may be one of several theories of creation and evolution taught. However, in some church-related schools, it may be the only version taught.

ESL: English as a Second Language differs from bilingual education because the emphasis is almost solely on teaching English.

Multiculturalism: Educating students about different cultures. A school, for example, may select textbooks and other materials that feature people from different cultures. Students may take part in projects that promote understanding of different cultures. In upper grades, a series of history lessons may be devoted to the study of many cultures.

Phonics: In reading and writing, using the sounds of letters and combinations of letters to determine how a word is spelled.

Values clarification: Rather than teaching specific values that all students are encouraged to adopt, this instruction helps students to analyze values and decide for themselves what ones will guide their thinking and behavior.

Videodisc: Combines print and video. For example, a disc might list the conditions that may cause a tornado to form and then show a tornado touching ground and swirling across the countryside.

Whole language: A system that combines reading and writing instruction. Students learn many words by using them in stories they compose. Also, students are encouraged to read good children's literature rather than just simple stories contained in basal readers.

DISCIPLINE

Corporal punishment: Physically striking a student, including slapping, paddling, or spanking. It is prohibited in public schools in many states.

Detention: For minor infractions, students may be required to attend a supervised "study hall" or stay briefly after school.

Due process: In cases where students are suspended or expelled, students and/or their parents may demand a hearing before appropriate school authorities and be represented by counsel of their choosing.

Expulsion: When a student is prohibited from coming to school for a number of weeks or months, or perhaps for an entire school year.

Suspension: This used to mean that a student would be prevented from coming to school for one or more days. However, in recent years, some schools have adopted "in-house suspension," whereby the student stays in school but is separated from his or her regular classes and usually remains in one room for all instruction.

Zero tolerance: Some secondary schools, plagued by violence and vandalism, have adopted this policy, whereby students who commit unlawful acts are immediately reported to the local police for appropriate action.

SPENDING

Bond issue: Public school districts generally raise large sums of money for school construction and major improvements by issuing bonds in specific amounts that are then purchased by investors in the open market.

Budget cap: Also known as *budget* or *spending ceiling,* it is a limit on how much a budget or spending can be increased.

Current expenditures: Money budgeted for instruction and other services that directly support students (includes salaries).

Capital outlay: Money budgeted for major repairs and renovations and new construction.

Debt service: Money budgeted to pay interest and principal on bond issues, major loans, and mortgages.

Formula aid: Sometimes called *foundation aid,* it is the basic state allotment a public school district may receive, exclusive of aid for special programs and purposes.

Ratable: Any property and structure within a taxing district that can be assessed for taxation. However, when school and municipal authorities refer to *ratables,* they are most often referring to business and industrial properties that substantially increase tax revenue.

STATISTICS

Average daily attendance (ADA): The actual attendance for the school year divided by the number of days school was in session.

Average daily membership (ADM): The number of students enrolled (membership) during the school year divided by the number of days school was in session.

Cohort: A group of students who have one or more statistical factors in common (e.g., age and grade).

Current expenditures per pupil in ADA: The total current expenditures budget divided by ADA. For example, if a school has budgeted $800,000 for current expenditures and the ADA is 400, the current expenditures per pupil would be $2,000.

Dropout rate: This statistic is figured a number of ways. One of the more common methods is the percentage of high school freshmen who do not graduate 4 years later.

STUDENTS

At-risk: Students who are most likely to fail in school because they may come from families in poverty or dysfunctional families, lack preparation for school, and/or have low self-esteem.

Emotionally disturbed: Characterized by an inability to learn that cannot be explained by any mental or physical problem, an inability to get along with others (but not necessarily disruptive), and long periods of unhappiness or depression.

Exceptional: May refer either to a student classified as gifted or one classified as handicapped.

Gifted: Schools may differ in their definition of who is gifted. In some schools, students must have an individually tested IQ of 120 or better. In others, students only need to demonstrate an above-average talent in music, art, etc., or have an above-average aptitude in a subject area, such as science or mathematics.

Individual educational plan (IEP): Required by federal law for students classified as handicapped, it may include special services the school must provide, as well as learning outcomes. Parents share in the creation of the IEP.

Learning disabled: Characterized by an unexplained inability to learn basic reading, writing, computation, and listening skills. Also may include students suffering from dyslexia (difficulty in reading and writing, often indicated by reversing letters in words).

Mentally retarded: Usually marked by an exceptionally low IQ for the student's age.

TEACHERS

Cognitive teaching: May be referred to as *cognitive strategies* or *cognitive learning.* Since the word *cognition* means to know or understand, cognitive teaching is primarily concerned with students' knowing or understanding information, concepts, etc.

For example instead of asking students merely to recite from memory facts and other information, the teacher might ask such probing questions as: Do you understand? What's your strategy?

Cooperative learning: The teacher divides the class into groups of three or four students each. Usually the students' desks are formed into a pod so that they face each other. Students work together on most lessons and projects.

Peer tutoring: When the teacher uses students to help other students who are having trouble learning certain skills.

Self-fulfilling prophecy: A theory that students often achieve as much or as little as teachers expect in advance. The term sometimes has been applied to a teacher who, expecting that certain students will not do well, offers them a level of instruction that may ensure they won't rise above the teacher's expectation.

Teaching to the test: A term usually used to fault teachers whose lesson plans are guided by tests given students. Many persons believe the criticism is unfair, since tests are designed to measure what students are supposed to have been taught and learned.

Team teaching: Two or more teachers share in leading a group of students. The team may include teachers of different subjects who have a common interest or create a common theme. For example, teachers of English and history (language arts and social studies in lower grades) and others might work together to instruct students about a certain historical period.

Time on task: The time students and teachers spend on activities intended to produce a particular learning outcome.

TESTING

Authentic assessment: Student achievement measured by performance. For example, writing skills may be tested by looking at a student's portfolio of written work. Higher-level math skills may be assessed according to how well a student can solve a problem. A student's knowledge of science may be tested by experiment or exhibit.

Competency test: A test developed by a state to find out how well a student has mastered the specific basic or advanced skills taught by the schools in that state. In many states, students must pass a competency test in order to graduate from high school.

Criterion-referenced test: Assesses an individual student's achievement.

Grade equivalency: A score used in reading assessment that usually consists of two numbers separated by a decimal point (5.3, 6.2, etc.). The first number refers to grade level and the second number refers to a month of the school year. If a fifth-grader receives a score of 6.2, for example, it means the student is reading fifth-grade material as well as a student in the second month of the sixth grade could.

Intelligence test: Measures a student's ability to learn and solve problems.

NAEP: The National Assessment of Educational Progress is a test sponsored by the federal government. It is given periodically to sample groups of students at ages 9, 13, and 17 (and also to adults aged 26). NAEP tests mastery of specific learning goals in reading, writing, mathematics, science, social studies, citizenship, music, literature, art, and career/occupational development. The results are often published to indicate the state of learning among American students.

Norm-referenced test: A standardized test (see definition in this category) that compares an individual's achievement with those of other students in the same school, district, and state, and usually with other students in the nation. The individual student's score usually is reported as a percentile. (See the definition of *percentile* in this category.) *Caution:* If you are simply told that *X* percent of students score above the national norm, be advised that the statistic may not be very significant. According to the U.S. Department of Education, "every state, and most [public school] districts, may be able to show you test results showing that their schools are above average." One reason for this phenomenon is that many tests set the norm very low.

Percentile: If a student ranks in the 80th percentile in reading, it means that the student has scored higher on the test than 80 percent of all students taking the test. However, there is no way of knowing how well the individual student actually did on the test. For example, 80 percent of other students taking the test may have correctly answered only half the test questions.

Scholastic Assessment Test (SAT): Note the change in name from Scholastic Aptitude Test. It is designed to show what a student has learned to date in various subject areas. Test questions are organized into two categories: verbal and mathematics. Many colleges have used the SAT as one way of assessing how well prepared a student is for college level work.

Standardized test: Any test that compares an individual student's performance with that of other students in a standard reference group (all students taking the same test). The standard reference group may include students of different ages and varying educational backgrounds.

Stanine: Compares an individual student's score with the scores of other students taking the same test. A stanine groups students according to their scores; there are nine stanines as follows: nine, top 4 percent; eight, next 7 percent; seven, next 12 percent; six, next 17 percent; five, middle 20 percent; four, next 17 percent; three, next 12 percent; two, next 7 percent; and one, lowest 4 percent.

PART 3

Evaluating an Elementary School

E lementary schools aren't what they used to be. Once upon a time most elementary schools started with kindergarten or grade 1 and ended with grade 6. Now, an elementary school might enroll preschool children and end at grade 4 or 5. In some public school districts, usually those attempting desegregation, there might even be a school for a single grade.

Whereas the old junior high school typically contained grades 7 to 9, today's middle school might be organized as grades 5 to 8, 6 to 8, 7 to 9, or some other combination.

For this section of the guidebook, I have settled on preschool or kindergarten through grade 6 as the definition of an elementary school. That means, naturally, Part 4, Evaluating a Secondary School, will be concerned with grades 7 to 12.

This part of the book is divided into five sections as follows:

1. *Parents, know your child.* In this section, parents are offered a series of questions they can use to evaluate their own child. The honest answers to the questions can help parents select the right school for their child.

2. *Questions you should ask.* This section includes a long list of questions parents should ask of school administrators, teachers, and other parents as they try to evaluate everything about a school, from how often textbooks are revised to how test scores are used to improve instruction.

3. *Observations you should make.* Not only do parents need to ask a number of questions when evaluating a school, but they also need to make some careful observations. This section tells parents what to look for.

4. *Data you should collect.* In order to complete a satisfactory evaluation of a school, parents need to collect important data. For example, parents checking out a

private/parochial school need to know not only what the cost is but also what financial aid is available. And all parents will want to obtain standardized test scores for a 3-year period and classroom teacher:student ratio.

5. *Workbook.* In the workbook, you have space to write answers to questions, observation notes, and data as you evaluate one, two, or three schools.

Parents, know your child

Every educator and parent whom I interviewed, or who has written about school evaluation, begins with child evaluation. The Carnegie Foundation for the Advancement of Teaching surveyed 7,000 kindergarten teachers in 1991 to find out what they looked for in children entering at that level. The survey questions focused on six areas: "physical well-being, social confidence, emotional maturity, language richness, general knowledge, and moral awareness." Those areas also can serve as the focus for questions parents should ask themselves about their child before entering the child at any grade level in any school.

Here are some questions you should answer about your child before evaluating or choosing an elementary school:

IS OUR CHILD IN REASONABLY GOOD HEALTH?

If your answer is not a firm Yes, you may want to seek a school with a well-trained, full-time medical/health staff, in a one-story building, perhaps a school that can provide good home instruction if your child is likely to miss class for days or weeks at a time because of a chronic ailment. If your child is in general good health but needs to lose weight or improve muscle tone, you may want a school where more attention is

paid to individual health and physical conditioning than to group sports.

HOW WELL DOES OUR CHILD GET ALONG WITH OTHERS?

Your answer may dictate the size of the school you choose or the average class size you want for your child. Depending on your answer, your child may profit from a school that favors open classrooms, cooperative learning, and team teaching. Or the child may need a very structured, traditional desks-in-a-row environment. Perhaps you want a school that encourages individual study.

IS OUR CHILD LESS MATURE THAN OTHER CHILDREN IN THE CHILD'S GRADE?

The problem of immaturity may begin when a child who has just turned 5 is accepted into kindergarten along with children who are almost 6. The child may remain slightly behind in maturity through the other grades. If this is so, you may want to select a school that will place your child in a classroom where most of the other students are at about the same maturity level. You also may want to ask a school's principal if the school has a policy regarding 1-year retention in grade for students who are immature. Emotional immaturity is one of the primary reasons why some students are retained in grade. However, recent research has shown that retention may lead to problems for the child later on. Therefore, you may want to ask the principal if the curriculum is flexible enough to adapt to the needs of an immature child.

A number of schools offer a transition experience, usually between kindergarten and first grade. This experience may be called *Kindergarten Plus* or *Pre-First Grade* or something else, but it is designed primarily to help the child who is ready to leave kindergarten but not quite mature enough for first grade.

HOW WELL DOES OUR CHILD COMMUNICATE THROUGH WRITING AND SPEAKING COMPARED TO OTHER CHILDREN OF THE SAME AGE AND GRADE LEVEL?

If your child reads very little at home, or was not read to very often in preschool years, and if your child seldom participates in family discussions and rarely if ever writes anything, chances are your child lacks adequate communication skills. Your assessment of your child usually will be confirmed by comments from teachers and grades on work turned in and tests given. If you feel your child is lacking basic communication skills, you may want to choose a school that stresses writing and speaking at all levels and offers remedial instruction. Also, some schools now assess a student's writing ability by looking at a portfolio of the student's essays and stories (see Testing: *authentic assessment*, in Part 2). The portfolio

is usually passed forward to the child's next teacher. Therefore, progress, or lack of it, can be noted.

If your child is an above-average communicator, for example has a more varied vocabulary than most of the child's friends, then you may want to seek out a school that offers many opportunities for students with advanced skills.

HOW MUCH GENERAL KNOWLEDGE DOES OUR CHILD HAVE?

As your child goes through the grades, you will have part of the answer from your examination of work the child brings home, parent-teacher conferences, and report cards. However, you also can take stock in other ways. For example: What is your child curious about? Can your child talk intelligently (for the child's age) about a wide range of topics? What books or publications does your child read?

WHAT MORAL VALUES DOES OUR CHILD HAVE?

You should know what values you have taught and modeled and how well your child reflects those values. Is your child secure enough in those values to withstand possible challenges from other students and teachers? You would be wise to look carefully at a school's statement about mission or goals. What does it say about moral and/or religious values? Then ask the school principal how the mission or goals are carried out and monitored.

Questions you should ask

Listed on the following pages are a number of questions you should ask school administrators and teachers and parents of children attending a school being evaluated. The questions are organized under various headings (e.g., Administration/Organization, Curriculum.

Part 4 includes workbook pages for you to use when you are evaluating a secondary school, but you can refer to them now. The questions listed here correspond to the questions listed in the workbook section. For example, it is suggested in this section, under the Administration/Organization heading, that you ask how many principals a school has had in the last 15 years. That question also will be listed under the same heading and in the same order in the workbook section (Part 4). If you ask that question and get an answer (e.g., "three"), you would write the answer in the appropriate spot.

You may be able to ask some or many of the questions at early spring parent orientation sessions conducted at the school(s) you are considering. In any event, it is always best to ask questions in person rather than over the telephone or by mail. Again, it is important to note that the questions, and later the observations, have been compiled after talking with school principals,

parents, and representatives of major education organizations. Nearly 700 principals from all parts of the nation responded to a survey that asked them to identify important questions parents should ask and observations they should make when evaluating an elementary school (see Appendix A).

Here are the questions to ask and the rationale for asking them:

ADMINISTRATION/ORGANIZATION

WHAT DOES THE SCHOOL'S MISSION STATEMENT SAY?

Rationale: Look at the mission statement carefully and question the principal closely about it. Are the statements merely good intentions and empty promises, or do they tell you much about the school, its philosophy, administration, teachers, and curriculum?

Here are some typical examples of mission statements that invite further questioning:

"Children are taught in a nurturing environment." (Might that mean much individual attention through very small classes, or average size or large classes that employ many aides?)

"Children are encouraged to learn through active, stimulating exploration." (Might that mean an education where children are learning mostly on their own and in small groups?)

"We believe all children are gifted and talented." (Undoubtedly correct in one sense, but does the school offer special instruction or individual study opportunities for gifted students as determined by IQ testing?)

"Our school cultivates the child intellectually and spiritually." (If this is a private school not affiliated with any particular religious denomination, what is the nature of the spiritual cultivation?)

"We are especially proud of our Emphasis on Character Program." (Is this a program separate from the regular curriculum, or is it built into all instruction? Is the emphasis on teaching certain values, and, if so, what are the values and how are they taught?)

HOW MANY PRINCIPALS HAS THE SCHOOL HAD IN THE PAST 15 YEARS?

Rationale: The principal is the school's instructional leader. As such, the principal is crucial to all that happens for and to your child. If the school has had more than four principals over the last 15 years, try to find out why. The reasons could be one or more of the following: friction among teachers or between teachers and the principals, the principals' dissatisfaction with policies of higher authority (superintendent or governing board), a clique of parents that interferes with school operations, or poor recruiting/screening procedures adopted by higher authority (a succession of mediocre principals has been hired). Also, the higher authority may have a policy of rotating principals frequently to bring in fresh ideas. While not necessarily a bad idea, the policy may overlook the fact that a principal

may take several years to "know" a school before even trying to make changes.

On the other hand, if the school has had the same principal for the last 15 years and perhaps longer, try to find out if the principal is still an energetic, creative leader. Teachers and parents are good sources to ask, but don't ask just one teacher or one parent. Because their comments will be subjective, you want to listen to more than one or two opinions. Also, see Section 3 for a suggested observation of the principal.

IS SCHOOL-BASED MANAGEMENT PRACTICED?

Rationale: Carefully question the principal, teachers, and other parents about this system (after reading the definition of the term *school-based management* in Part 2). School-based management is generally considered a good thing, but as with many other trends in education, it can also be the "in" thing to do. Therefore, some principals are apt to answer glibly that their school practices school-based management when it doesn't, or only in some minor way. "Although there are some school[s]...which appear to be practicing various forms of school-based management, few...fit the demanding definition...," wrote consultant Richard G. Neal in his book *School-Based Management.*

To be real school-based management, according to Neal, "at least 75 percent of the entire [public or private] school system's operating budget should be spent by the [schools in the system.]" Some schools that claim they are into school-based management may have much less control over spending. School-based management also demands that goal setting and decisions be truly shared by the principal, teachers, and parents. Together they design an education plan in keeping with the overall goals of the board that governs the school. "For example," wrote Neal, "one goal...might describe how the school intends to carry out the school board goal to improve reading skills and comprehension...Another goal...might be devoted to [an] objective [unrelated to the system's goals] to beautify the front entrance of the school."

If in response to your questions, the principal says, for example, that all teachers have an opportunity to submit budget requests and that a curriculum committee reviews curriculum in one or more subjects each year, the school probably does *not* practice school-based management.

IS THE SCHOOL ENGAGED IN RESTRUCTURING?

Rationale: Read the definition in Part 2 before asking. As with school-based management, a principal may claim restructuring when it really doesn't exist. Ask the principal, teachers, and parents if changes made in the school are primarily designed to benefit students. "The important element [in restructuring] is the emphasis on ensuring that student learning remains the key variable that is being affected through the proposed changes," wrote David T. Corley in a series of books titled *Trends and Issues.* "It is easy for this goal to become obscured in the discussion of various changes that may

really make schools better places for adults, not students." For example, if the principal cites school-based management as an example of restructuring, it is not. Because it is a management system, students benefit only indirectly.

WHAT IS THE SCHOOL'S TEACHING PHILOSOPHY?

Rationale: The 700 elementary school principals surveyed considered this to be one of the top 10 questions parents should ask (ranked sixth). Another way to put this question is to ask how students and teachers are organized. Here are some of the possibilities (also refer back to the glossary, Part 2): highly structured, open education, and cooperative learning.

Some schools, of course, have all three formats going at one time, leaving the choices up to individual teachers or teachers of a certain grade. For example, teachers in first through third grades may opt for highly structured classrooms, while teachers in the upper grades are experimenting with cooperative learning.

After you get your answer (and also observe various philosophies or patterns in operation), you should line up that information alongside the answers you gave to the questions about your child (Section 1). The last thing parents should do, for example, is to place their slightly immature child, who is reluctant to work with others, into a highly charged environment.

WHAT IS THE SCHOOL'S HOMEWORK POLICY?

Rationale: If the school has a written policy, check it against this advice contained in *Educators Handbook* (Virginia Richardson Koehler, senior editor):

> The most defensible statement to make about homework is that if assigned in some sensible quantity, if tied to the curriculum, if success is possible or diagnostic information can be derived, and if feedback is regularly provided, homework will be of great [value] to teachers and students.

If the school's policy recommends a certain amount of time for homework each day, ask how the time was arrived at. Also, the amount of time spent on homework should vary. For example, the "sensible quantity" of homework for a student in the first grade should be less than that expected of a sixth-grader.

If the school has no written policy, ask the principal to explain whether teachers regularly assign, check, grade, and return homework.

WHAT IS THE POLICY ON PLACING PHYSICALLY CHALLENGED AND GIFTED CHILDREN?

Rationale: Schools must be guided by federal law (Handicapped Education Act and American Disabilities Act)) and state regulations when classifying physically and mentally challenged children and deciding what educational and support services they should receive. However, the school may be free to decide whether to teach most physically challenged students in special or regular classrooms (mainstreaming or inclusion). No federal law and, in most cases, no state regulations apply to gifted students. Some schools place gifted students in regular classes all of the time. Other schools have a pull-out program in which gifted students are in regular classes most of the day but may be pulled out for an hour or two of special instruction or individual study and research.

DOES THE SCHOOL OFFER HEAD START AND/OR CHAPTER 1 PROGRAMS?

Rationale: If you believe your child can profit from one or both of these federally funded programs, do not assume that every school offers them. Some schools do not qualify, or they choose not to participate. If the school does have one or both programs, ask what the criteria are for inclusion. Does your child qualify?

HAS THE SCHOOL DEVISED LEARNING OUTCOMES?

Rationale: Teachers should know what children in their classroom are supposed to learn by the end of the year (grade). Each teacher may act alone to devise learning outcomes, but it is more likely that outcomes are decided by groups of teachers, usually organized according to grade level. Setting outcomes also may be a part of school-based management, as principal, teachers, and parents set the means for achieving goals in their educational plan. Ask to see goals and learning outcomes for the grade level where your child will be placed.

WHAT SPECIAL SERVICES DOES THE SCHOOL OFFER?

Rationale: Depending upon your and your child's needs, you may want to know about such special services or programs as the following:

- Before-school or after-school tutoring
- After-school child care

- Health care, counseling, or other assistance that might be provided by municipal or regional social agencies before or after school.

It is important to ask how to qualify for such programs, the hours offered, and how programs are supervised.

WHAT IS THE SCHOOL'S POLICY REGARDING WHO MAY CONTACT YOUR CHILD DURING SCHOOL HOURS OR AFTER SCHOOL?

Rationale: If you are a single parent with a court order that gives you sole custody of your child and which even may specifically prevent the other parent from unauthorized contact with the child, make sure the school has a clear-cut policy concerning such situations. You will want answers to at least these questions:

- Are all visitors required to report to the main office?
- Are office personnel familiar with court orders filed in the office, and do they honor such orders to the letter?
- Have teachers been instructed not to release a child to any adult unless that person has been cleared by the office?
- Have teachers or other personnel responsible for monitoring children leaving school at the end of the day been briefed on the person or persons authorized to pick up children?

ADMISSIONS

WHAT ARE THE REQUIREMENTS FOR ADMISSION?

Rationale: This is especially important for students considering an indepen-

dent or private school. However, public schools also have their criteria. Here is a list of information you may want to obtain:

Age minimums and maximums. For example, school policy may vary on the minimum age for admission to kindergarten.

Entrance tests. Some private/independent schools may require diagnostic testing or other tests prior to acceptance.

Health certification. The school may require proof of certain vaccinations. In some cases, results of a recent physical examination must be provided. Also, a school may require a detailed history of previous and existing illnesses, conditions, and disabilities.

Interviews. The school may require interviews with parents and students. Such interviews, for example, may help decide whether a student is ready for an open classroom, whether the student needs instruction in English as a second language, whether the student should be excused from certain activities, and so on.

Letters of recommendation. Some schools with a religious affiliation, for example, may require such a letter from a student's pastor or spiritual leader.

WHAT ORIENTATION PROGRAM IS OFFERED PARENTS AND STUDENTS, AND WHEN IS IT SCHEDULED?

Rationale: Most schools provide some kind of orientation. Such a program is often a good time to ask questions and make observations (if a building tour is included). If you are in a public school district where there is great diversity among individual schools, a general orientation that provides information about the various schools and their teaching philosophy, curriculum, and other characteristics would be helpful. If the district offers magnet schools, for example, you need to know about each school's specialty and also about the quality of its basic curriculum. Typically, the most inclusive orientation programs are offered in the early spring.

WHAT SCHOLARSHIPS AND OTHER FINANCIAL AID ARE AVAILABLE?

Rationale: Several options are available at most private schools. These may include scholarships funded by private individuals, corporations, organizations, religious institutions, foundations, and the school itself.

Available aid packages may be given on the basis of family income or merit, or both. The school also may arrange an extended payment plan or suggest how loans may be obtained. Ask to talk with the school's financial aid officer.

CURRICULUM

WHAT KNOWLEDGE AND SKILLS SHOULD AN ELEMENTARY SCHOOL BE TEACHING, OR, TO PUT IT ANOTHER AND PERHAPS BETTER WAY, WHAT KNOWLEDGE AND SKILLS SHOULD A STUDENT IN ELEMENTARY SCHOOL BE LEARNING?

This may be the mother of all questions, and it is probably directed at educators in general rather than to the principal of a particular school you are evaluating. However, the answer can help you ask other questions concerning curriculum goals and learning outcomes at the school you are considering.

As the nation rushes toward the 21st century, the pace also quickens toward national curriculum standards, a national curriculum, and probably one national testing system. Presently, however, it is possible to attend public or private schools in different parts of the country, state, county, and, even, municipality and discover that all children are not being taught the same knowledge and skills. Some persons argue that diversity is a good thing, and they probably are right when it comes to the methods of teaching and learning and even the timetable for teaching certain knowledge and skills. However, more and more educators and laypersons are discovering that the world of today, let alone tomorrow, requires of everybody a certain level of knowledge and skill development that was not deemed so crucial even as recently as when many of today's parents were themselves in the lower grades.

By the time you are reading this book, national curriculum standards are scheduled for completion in these subject areas: mathematics, science, history, the arts, civics and government, geography, English and language arts (communication skills), and foreign languages. Appendix B advises where you might find out more about these standards.

Many educators believe, however, that at least a framework for determining what knowledge and skills children need already exists. Twenty-five years ago, the federal government created the National Assessment of Educational Progress (NAEP). The government wanted to know the level of "educational achievement" in the subjects listed above by students in the fourth, eighth and twelfth grades. In order to carry out its assignment, NAEP (developed by Educational Testing Service) had to pick the minds of top educators in all those subject areas to find out what they thought students should have learned by the time they reached those grade levels. The consensus of all those educators became the framework for questions NAEP has used ever since to sample periodically "educational achievement" by students in public and private schools. NAEP's periodic report often has been called the *nation's report card.*

Educational Testing Service has provided this question framework for major subjects included in this book. It can be found in Appendix B, along with further explanations.

HOW IS CURRICULUM DECIDED?

Rationale: In some states, much of the public school curriculum is dictated by the state education department. This curriculum may consist mostly of general requirements for the teaching of reading, writing, and computation skills, but the state also may demand that a specific amount of time be spent on certain subjects and skills. It may even provide actual lesson plans. The state may compose curriculum and mandate instruction on such matters as AIDS, bicycle safety, dental health, drugs, environment, nutrition, self-esteem, sex, and a host of other subjects. Elementary school teachers in some states, for example, are directed to spend 10 or 15 minutes a day having their students wash out their mouth with fluoride.

Most states have their own competency tests (see glossary, Part 2), and these tests, along with standardized achievement tests, help decide curriculum in public schools. For example, if the tests emphasize some skills and downplay others, the local school curriculum will likely do the same.

If school-based management is in place, the principal, teachers, and parents are playing a major role in devising curriculum when the state or governing body has supplied only general goals or guidelines. Even where school-based management is not practiced, teacher committees may be formed to write and review curriculum according to grade level or subject.

The curriculum of private schools associated with a particular religion, denomination, or church is, of course, heavily influenced by religious beliefs. For example, whereas a public school may have sex education from kindergarten on up through the grades, the private school with a religious influence may offer no sex education. Also, greater censorship may be practiced in literature, social studies, science, and the arts.

On the other hand, most other private schools have considerable freedom in the design of curriculum. A school's governing board may draft general curriculum guidelines, but the principal and teachers usually are free to decide how the goals will be implemented. Therefore, such a private school is most likely to be creative and experimental in what is taught and how it is taught.

Important note: Regardless of what school you are evaluating, you should ask to examine curriculum and learning outcomes of special interest or concern to you. For example, you may want to know what your third-grader is going to learn about sexual relationships. You may want to find out if students are taught to review and revise their writing, or whether they are simply encouraged to express themselves and worry about correcting the expression at some later date or grade. Be suspicious of any school that refuses your request to examine curriculum and learning outcomes.

HOW OFTEN ARE CURRICULUM AND TEXTBOOKS REVIEWED AND UPDATED?

Rationale: The elementary school principals ranked this question among the top 10 questions parents should ask. The school should have a schedule for curriculum review. Ask about it. Be suspicious of any school that has no schedule, or if curriculum review is conducted less frequently than every 5 years. Also, be wary of any school where teachers are not involved in curriculum review or where there is little opportunity for teachers' views on curriculum to be heard and acted upon.

Textbooks in mathematics, science, and social studies ideally should be replaced at least every 5 years. Otherwise, new knowledge and information based on recent development, experience, and research may not be included. Many educators warn parents to stay clear of schools where textbooks in those subjects are older than 10 years.

DOES THE READING PROGRAM BALANCE PHONICS AND WHOLE LANGUAGE INSTRUCTION? (LOOK UP THOSE TERMS IN THE GLOSSARY, PART 2.)

Rationale: Nothing is quite so controversial in elementary education as the method(s) for teaching children how to read and comprehend what they read. Some educators argue that phonics alone is the secret to decoding words and learning to read. Some others say children will not really learn to read and comprehend unless they see how words appear on the printed page and then use those words in their own writing.

A growing number of educators, however, now believe that the best approach to teaching reading is a combination of phonics and whole language. These educators also generally agree that children learning to read must have access to a variety of good literature: classic and contemporary books.

An important part of your evaluation is to obtain and compare test data that indicate reading achievement over a period of several years (see Section 4).

DOES THE SCHOOL HAVE A WELL-EQUIPPED AND WELL-USED LIBRARY/MEDIA CENTER?

Rationale: This question also was ranked among the top 10 by the elementary school principals. The principals obviously agree with the American Association of School Libraries, whose credo is that "the school library media program that is fully integrated into the school's curriculum is central to the learning process." The association urges that libraries reflect and complement a school's curriculum with a full range of print and audiovisual materials. These materials should include books, newspapers, magazines, videodiscs, laser discs, videotapes, computer discs, films, film strips, audiocassettes, and audio compact discs, plus the equipment for using them, if the equipment is not located in the classrooms. The association also recommends that the library be staffed by at least one full-time library media specialist.

Elementary school students should be trained to discover what print and audiovisual materials are available to them, how to analyze and select the materials they want, and how to use them. Also, students should have frequent and regular access to the library. Adequate seating should be available.

Especially in the lower elementary grades, students often go to the library as a class. Older students may go to the library on their own or in small groups. In either case, students need enough time to find and use the materials. There are no specific guidelines as to how much time students should spend in the library on any one occasion, but many teachers find that at least 45 minutes are needed for a class visit.

HOW ARE COMPUTERS USED FOR INSTRUCTION?

Rationale: Once upon a very short time ago, the computer was a school oddity. Twelve years ago, a national survey reported 250,000 sets in all of America's public elementary and secondary schools. Where they did exist, they were used mostly for remedial instruction in reading comprehension and mathematics. Today, the computer has become an important—some would say indispensable—educational tool. Five years ago, the estimated number of computers in schools already had risen to 2 million. The number in public schools today is far in excess of the 1990 figure. The National Governors' Association (NGA) reported in 1991 that the ratio of students to computers was 20:1.

Many public and private elementary schools now have computer labs where students, typically by the second or third grade, are taught how to use a computer. Most schools also have at least one computer per classroom, beginning again by the second or third grade. Computers now are used for such activities as writing and editing essays, solving problems in mathematics and science, and locating a wide variety of encyclopedic information and other valuable source material. The NGA reported in 1991 that at least 10,000 programs were then available for use in schools.

In some schools, students using computers in their classroom may tap into programs stored in the school library, perhaps even other libraries in the area. Also, in some schools, students are able to communicate with each other via computer, and communicate with a wide range of persons and places outside the school and the community. Teachers may have their own computer for research and lesson preparation.

If the school you are evaluating has a student:computer ratio in excess of 25:1, and if software for use in the computers is scarce, ask whether the school has plans for adding computers and software.

DOES THE SCHOOL TEACH VALUES?

Rationale: Regarding values clarification (see glossary, Part 2), the U.S.

Department of Education reported the following in 1988:

> Much research has been done in the last 20 years or so to measure the effects of this approach. The various studies consistently conclude that, according to all measures considered, values clarification does not appear to have any effect at all.

Therefore, if the school you are evaluating boasts of "teaching" values clarification, ask the principal or teachers to explain what the school means by the term and if the school has any reliable means for assessing the worth of the instruction.

Increasingly, public schools are content with urging students and teachers to behave in an ethical and moral manner toward each other. The standards (sometimes published) might include, for example: honesty; rules that are fair to all; tolerance for persons of different races, colors, cultures, and religious views; and respect for public and private property.

Supreme Court decisions have ruled out prayer and other religious exercises in public schools, but the Court has suggested that public schools teach about religions. Nothing prevents a public school, therefore, from teaching about the beliefs and values of various religious faiths and how they have affected the life of people and countries.

Private schools, particularly those affiliated with a religion or church, may teach specific beliefs and values. For example, the independent Chicago Junior School, which is not affiliated with any religion or religious institution, states: "Our curriculum is enhanced by our Character Building Program, emphasizing qualities such as honesty, discipline, and creativity."

DISCIPLINE

WHAT IS THE SCHOOL'S DISCIPLINE POLICY?

Rationale: You will want to know what offenses the school considers grounds for punishment and what punishments are authorized. Also, you will want to be assured that the school knows what your and your child's rights are regarding discipline. This question also was on the principals' top-10 list.

In his book *You Can Improve Your Child's School,* William Rioux and the staff of the former National Committee for Citizens in Education (NCCE) tell of a sixth-grader who received an hour's detention after school for accidentally dropping a book on the floor. While no disciplinary policy can possibly anticipate all situations where some form of punishment is in order, the rules should be specific enough so that teachers and parents can properly instruct and warn students about punishable behavior.

Detention (time usually spent in the principal's office or elsewhere during or after school), denial of privileges and taking part in extracurricular activities, suspension, and expulsion (in order of severity) are typical punishments.

In some states, public school teachers may administer corporal punishment for misbehavior, for example spanking or paddling. However, such physical punishment (except to protect someone from being injured or killed) is outlawed in these states: Alaska, Arkansas, California, Connecticut, District of

Columbia, Hawaii, Iowa, Maine, Massachusetts, Michigan, Minnesota, Montana, Nebraska, New Hampshire, New Jersey, New York, North Dakota, Oregon, Rhode Island, South Dakota, Vermont, Virginia, and Wisconsin. The National Association of Elementary School Principals has voted to ban corporal punishment.

Disciplinary policies and practices of private schools, of course, often are not covered by any state guidelines or regulations.

You should know that in most states parents of public school students have these specific rights regarding the discipline of their child:

- To take legal action against teachers and administrators who use "excessive or unreasonable" physical force.
- To appeal a suspension or expulsion.
- To appeal a decision to place their child in a class or building designed and labeled for "disruptive" children (see Administration Organization *alternative school* in the glossary, Part 2).

MAINTENANCE

DOES THE SCHOOL BUDGET ALLOW FOR REGULAR CUSTODIAL AND MAINTENANCE SERVICE AND PROMPT REPAIRS?

Rationale: When budgets have to be cut, custodial and maintenance service and repairs are often the first targets. You should ask school officials if the governing body has adequately funded custodial and maintenance services and repairs over the last 3 years. Also ask whether the school is presently in need

of custodial and maintenance personnel, services, or repairs. You also might want to ask about contracts with custodial and maintenance personnel. Are such workers hired on the basis of experience and ability, or because of seniority in a union or political connections? A good contract should require custodial and maintenance personnel to be trained as necessary in new procedures and the use of new equipment.

PARENT/COMMUNITY INVOLVEMENT

TO WHAT DEGREE ARE SCHOOL PARENTS AND OTHER LAYPERSONS INVITED TO HELP DECIDE BUDGET, CURRICULUM, PERSONNEL, ND OTHER POLICIES?

Rationale: Parent/community participation varies widely, even among public schools in a single district and among private schools in a community or region. It is not uncommon, for example, for parents in one public school to be very active in decision making and to be nearly shut out in a school across town. One school may have a dynamic, influential parent organization, while another spends most of its time running bake sales and most of its money buying equipment that should be in the school's budget. However, increasingly across the country school officials are relying on parent/community advice and consent regarding important policies and regulations. Two major movements previously discussed, school-based management and restructuring, depend on strong, consistent parent/community involvement.

Inquire whether parents serve on standing committees that make or review policy, or whether parents and community leaders are called together only when an issue gets too hot for school officials to handle alone.

Talk to several parents of children already attending the school you are evaluating. If you don't know any, ask the school to supply a list of officers and members of the school parent organization. You also might want to talk with officers or members of the local League of Women Voters (LWV) or Association of University Women. These people usually can provide you with honest, yet subjective, answers to your questions about not only parental involvement but other aspects of the school as well.

HOW WELL DOES THE SCHOOL COMMU-NICATE WITH PARENTS/COMMUNITY THROUGH PUBLICATIONS AND THE MEDIA?

Rationale: Most private schools, with the possible exception of some church-related schools or others controlled by a central authority, are solely responsible for communicating with their own parents and other selected audiences (e.g., parents of prospective students and news media). On the other hand, most public schools, while they may have their own publications, usually rely on the district office for the preparation and distribution of information to news media and newsletters and other publications to parents/community.

You should find out the nature of publications sent home by the school and any central office, how often they are sent, and by what means. If the school (central office) newsletter is issued less often than quarterly, it is not doing a very good job of informing

the people. If the newsletter and occasional flyers are sent by way of the students, beware the "lost-enroute theory." It goes something like this: The older the child, the less likely the child will deliver to parents whatever the school has sent home.

Examine several issues of the newsletter. Are they mostly filled with such inconsequential notes as the report that Ms. Smith's class cut out Thanksgiving turkeys for the tenth year in a row? Or do they include well-written, informative articles reporting such developments as a revision of the social studies curriculum and the purchase of CD-ROM computers and science software? Also, check to see if the newsletter is primarily a vehicle for the principal. Does the principal write nearly everything? Is most space devoted to the principal's message, a pep talk, or self-serving report of unspecified "continued progress?"

IN WHAT OTHER WAYS DOES THE SCHOOL COMMUNICATE TO PARENTS/COMMUNITY?

Rationale: Schools and central authorities that are really serious about good communication are likely to use one or more of these means:

> *Focus groups.* A term borrowed from the field of public relations, it refers to small groups that are called together to discuss, evaluate, and criticize ideas and proposals.
>
> *Cable television.* In many areas of the country, cable TV companies have reserved at least one channel for community use.

Key communicators. In every neighborhood, community, and region, there are people who, because of their job and/or their personality, talk with a great many other people every day. These communicators might include a barber or hairdresser, service station owner, store clerk, secretary, restaurant hostess, school custodian, and police officer. The communicators are especially helpful in picking up potentially damaging rumors on the one hand and passing along facts on the other.

Surveys. Some schools and central authorities send out questionnaires on a regular basis to obtain feedback from parents and others on issues facing the school (schools).

HOW OFTEN ARE PARENT-TEACHER CONFERENCES SCHEDULED?

Rationale: Most schools schedule at least two conferences a year, one each semester. Also, if daytime hours are generally inconvenient because of work, ask if at least one round of conferences is scheduled at night. An increasing number of schools do have night conferences.

IS IT POSSIBLE TO MEET WITH TEACHERS AT TIMES OTHER THAN SCHEDULED CONFERENCES?

Rationale: Occasionally you may have questions or suggestions concerning your child that simply can't wait for a scheduled conference. Therefore, it's important to know if teachers are available at other reasonable times. Also, check to see what the school's procedure is for contacting a teacher.

CAN YOU OBSERVE YOUR CHILD'S CLASS IN SESSION?

Rationale: Some schools are very reluctant to allow parents to observe their child's class, alleging that the parents might embarrass their child and/or disrupt the class. Other schools welcome an occasional classroom visit by parents. I know of at least one school where parents are also encouraged to come to school and have lunch with their child. In some schools, classroom visitations are subject to contract negotiation. Find out the policy at the school you are evaluating.

Some states have laws or regulations that spell out the parents' right to visit their child's classroom during school hours if they first notify the school office. These states are Alabama, Alaska, Arizona, District of Columbia, Florida, Indiana, Iowa, Maine, Maryland, Nevada, New Hampshire, New Mexico, North Carolina, North Dakota, Ohio, Oklahoma, and Texas. However, a majority of public and private schools in all states have a policy that permits such visits.

SECURITY
WHAT IS THE SCHOOL POLICY ON SECURITY?

Rationale: School policy should ensure students' security as they arrive at school, during school hours, and when they leave school. The policy, then, should provide for monitoring bus/car drop-off and pick-up points, all entrances, hallways, and play areas. If security personnel are employed, the policy should spell out their duties. The policy also should tell how school officials determine the purpose of visitors.

STUDENTS

HOW ARE STUDENTS CLASSIFIED AS GIFTED?

Rationale: If your child is intellectually gifted (perhaps the child was so classified at another school), make sure you find out how the school you are evaluating identifies gifted students.

Glossary entries in Part 2 have already put you on notice that schools may have very different standards. For example, some educators, for philosophical or political reasons, want nearly all students to be considered gifted. This may be true in the sense that every human being is more capable of learning some things and accomplishing some tasks than others. But other educators, and many parents, argue that a student who is more able to solve math problems than write essays, for example, is not necessarily gifted in mathematics.

If you believe your child to be intellectually gifted, you should probably have the child's IQ individually tested and then find a school that relies on IQ scores, other assessment data, teacher recommendations, and parent testimony regarding early development and home experience as bases for classifying gifted students.

HOW ARE STUDENTS DIAGNOSED AS EMOTIONALLY DISTURBED OR LEARNING DISABLED?

Rationale: Large numbers of students in some public schools are so diagnosed. Many educators and parents are very critical of some special education classification. "When children cannot meet the expectations of a norm-bound curriculum," warned Patte Barth and Ruth Mitchell in their book *Smart Start,* "the school responds by putting them into low, remedial tracks or even into special education classes." The authors cited the case of 8-year-old "Jorge," whose teacher wanted him diagnosed as learning disabled because he sometimes reversed written figures and was reluctant to read out loud. Once children are so diagnosed, they often are never reevaluated. Barth and Mitchell claim that many of these children are thus "programmed for failure."

Whether or not you fear your child might be misdiagnosed, you would be well to check with the school principal on how children are diagnosed. If the school routinely diagnoses students as learning disabled or emotionally disturbed primarily on teacher recommendations, be suspicious of how teachers and administrators in that school treat students in general. Also, ask whether students' special needs are reexamined on a regular basis. What incentive or hope exists for students who know they have almost no chance of ever moving up to a higher track?

DO STUDENTS HAVE THE RIGHT TO AVOID SOME CONTROVERSIAL CURRICULUM ON THE ONE HAND BUT EMBRACE SOME CONTROVERSIAL OPINIONS OR GROUPS ON THE OTHER?

Rationale: Roughly half the states have laws or regulations that excuse students in public schools from studying subjects, reading books, or taking part in activities that they or their parents object to on religious, moral, or other reasonable grounds. Ask the principal about the policy in the public or private school you are evaluating.

Public school students (and their parents) in all states except Arkansas, Colorado, Kentucky, Michigan, Minnesota, Missouri, New Mexico, Tennessee, Vermont, and Wisconsin have a right to appeal any local policy that prevents them from expressing controversial views. Of course, the protection does not extend to views that are libelous, slanderous, obscene, or likely to cause serious disruption. Laws or regulations in most states also allow students (or their parents) to appeal any local decision that prevents students from joining clubs and organizations that are controversial but otherwise lawful.

TEACHERS

WHAT IS THE SCHOOL'S PROGRAM FOR STAFF DEVELOPMENT AND CONTINUING EDUCATION FOR TEACHERS?

Rationale: This question was voted by the principals surveyed as one of the ten most essential. The reason it is so important is that teachers and other staff personnel need ongoing assistance in several ways:

- To become aware of the latest research and experience that affects subject matter, teaching methods, and student learning
- To be trained to use new curriculum and teaching methods
- To deal with problems that interfere with effective teaching and learning
- To improve teachers' ability to communicate effectively with each other, administrators, students, and parents

Staff development is carried on primarily within the school or school system. Continuing education usually means attending classes at a nearby college. Often, a school or school system will pay a teacher's tuition for continuing education. Also, additional college credits and degrees generally lead to higher salaries.

You would be wise to ask a couple of teachers about staff development in addition to asking the principal or administrator in charge of the program. The teachers could tell you whether staff development is meeting their specific needs or whether the program deals mainly with general information about "education reform" and "social problems."

ARE SUCH SUBJECTS AS MUSIC, ART, PHYSICAL EDUCATION, AND HEALTH TAUGHT BY SPECIALISTS?

Rationale: It has been common practice in public schools to sacrifice the arts and physical education if spending is tight. When this happens, specialists' positions may be eliminated. Even in public school systems where the arts have survived the budget ax, specialists may be spread thin. They may visit a school infrequently.

The standard set for elementary schools by the Music Educators' National Conference is one music specialist for every 400 students to maintain a bare-bones program. A quality program is one specialist for every 265 students.

If the arts and physical education are taught by classroom teachers in the school you are looking at, ask what training they have in the subjects and how much time is devoted to them.

Remember, having students cut out pumpkins is not necessarily art instruction, and opening the day with a little song is not music instruction.

DOES THE SCHOOL HAVE REGULAR ACCESS TO SUCH PROFESSIONALS AS LIBRARIAN, PSYCHOLOGIST, COUNSELOR, THERAPIST, AND NURSE?

Rationale: A quality elementary school not only has a well-stocked library but also a librarian to run it and help students and teachers. A psychologist needs to be available to examine students with learning and emotional problems and to aid in some test construction and analysis. Many parents think of counselors at the secondary level, but an increasing number of elementary schools employ a counselor. The counselor may serve some of the same functions as a psychologist and also may guide students toward curricular choices in secondary school.

Some schools employ a therapist to help students with a speech impairment. A nurse, of course, is needed to tend to students who have a health problem or get hurt. The nurse may be called upon to monitor students who are taking prescribed drugs.

Particularly in small schools, most or all of these specialists may be employed part-time.

ARE THERE TEACHER AIDES?

Rationale: Teacher aides, who may be paid professionals or volunteer parents, are helpful in several ways, particularly in classes with 18 or more students. First, they take over some clerical duties, thus enabling the teacher to spend more time working with individuals and small groups. Second, they can help maintain classroom order. Also, especially in the lower grades, they can assist in satisfying students' needs. For example, a child has a bathroom emergency, another has trouble adjusting to school, and several children have trouble getting in and out of winter coats and leggings.

TESTING

WHAT TESTS ARE GIVEN, AND HOW ARE THE RESULTS USED?

Rationale: Most elementary schools use standardized achievement tests and teacher-made tests. Common standardized achievement tests are the Iowa Tests of Basic Skills, the Metropolitan Achievement Tests, and California Achievement Tests. These tests measure (1) how well students have learned the basic skills and (2) knowledge the educators believe they should have learned by a certain age or grade.

One problem with using these tests is that students and their teachers can appear to be inept if, for example, their school elects to teach some skills in the fifth grade that the test-makers thought should have been learned by the end of the fourth grade. Also, of course, national tests do not take into account individual differences. For example, it may take student A longer than students B and C to learn fractions. On the other hand, student A may be ahead of his peers in sentence composition. One way good schools use test results is to reevaluate curriculum and teaching methods. For example, if the standardized test showed that many students had not mastered skills their teachers had taught them, then there may be something wrong with the instruction. Perhaps textbooks are too old. Maybe more drill is necessary.

Also, a national test may point out that some skills or knowledge not thought by local teachers to be very important are obviously considered vital by most other schools. Many families moving from one state to another, or even within a state, have found that students in the new school are either ahead or behind their child. Therefore, local teachers may decide to revise their instruction to ensure that their students are in the "mainstream."

HOW ARE TEST RESULTS REPORTED TO PARENTS?

Rationale: The school should advise parents how their child fared on any given test. Also, parents should know how well their child's class and school did by comparison to state and national results. The results should be reported in language parents can understand, and the school should say how it will use the results.

TRANSPORTATION

WHAT IS THE TRANSPORTATION POLICY?

Rationale: Public school policies vary. For example, in one school district all kindergarten children may be bused, regardless of where they live, but other children are bused only if they reside a certain distance from school or live along a highway where walking is considered hazardous. In some places, public school buses will transport children to a private school if both the child and the school are located on an existing public school bus route.

In some cases, a public school bus also will take a child to a private day care center after school if the parents are unable to pick up the child until later in the day. Again, this depends on the location of the school and available seats on the bus.

Some private schools have their own bus service, but in many instances parents are responsible for transporting their child to and from school. In some cases, you may want to ask about car pools. Some private day schools are located on beautiful campuses, but isolated from most housing in the region and far removed from main roads. Choosing such a school, then, often depends on whether an existing car pool serves the area where you live.

Be sure to find out about the rules on bus behavior. Some parents have been surprised, for example, to learn that their child has been prohibited from riding the bus after committing two minor infractions. Many schools have become very tough about student misbehavior on buses, because the safety of all children depends on how well the bus driver can control the operation of the bus. If one or two students interfere with safe operation, all students are in jeopardy.

Observations you should make

DO STUDENTS SEEM TO BE ACTIVELY INVOLVED IN LEARNING?

Of the 700 principals who responded to our survey, 467 chose as the most essential action parents can take in evaluating a school the observation of classrooms to see if students are actively involved in learning.

First, do not even consider a school where you are not allowed to observe classrooms in session. That doesn't mean you go into every classroom and wander around while learning is going on, nor should you feel entitled to sit or stand in a classroom for a long period, thereby distracting students and teacher. However, you should be able to look into a number of classrooms briefly and get a sense of what is going on.

Here are some guidelines on spotting "actively involved" learning:

- Students in most classrooms are either asking questions of the teacher, engaged in discussion with other students, working on a group project, or working on their own.
- Students in most classrooms are not sitting at desks in rows.
- Work stations exist where small groups of students can work together (cooperative learning)

or be helped by the teacher or aide.

- A variety of learning tools other than textbooks are available to students in most classrooms. These should include computers and appropriate software, other print materials, audiotapes, and self-instructional "packages."

DO TEACHERS MANAGE THE CLASSROOM EFFECTIVELY?

In the past, it was said that a teacher was managing the classroom if the school visitor walking down hallways heard hardly a sound from classrooms except for the soothing voice of teachers teaching. As indicated by the guidelines above, if students are actively involved in learning, there is going to be noise. Occasionally, it may even be loud.

However, it doesn't take an expert to tell the difference between the "good noise" of learning and the "bad noise" of students out of control. Learning noise is orchestrated by the teacher; disruptive noise is not. The excited talk of students engaged in an experiment or other project is not easily confused with babble about a favorite TV sitcom, rock band, or video game. Nor is it hard to distinguish spirited debate from undisciplined argument.

IS STUDENTS' WORK PROMINENTLY DISPLAYED IN CLASSROOMS AND ON THE WALLS OF CORRIDORS?

A school that prefers to show off its tastefully painted walls or store-bought art over students' work is a school to walk out of. Where active learning is going on, where students are engaged in creating, their work will cover the walls. However, a word of caution from a wise parent: A wall plastered exclusively with pictures of the same scene (e.g., family members, flowers, Halloween pumpkins) is less indicative of creative teachers and students than walls displaying a variety of scenes and themes.

ARE VISITORS, ESPECIALLY PARENTS, WARMLY WELCOMED?

If you get a little shiver up your spine when you walk into a school and are greeted by a sign that reads "ALL visitors MUST report to the main office," pay attention to the shiver. Security is important, especially nowadays, and schools correctly do not want strangers prowling the halls. However, the sign referred to is not going to discourage someone up to no good, and the sign might symbolize that the school is not eager to welcome any visitor, including parents. It is no guarantee, of course, but you and your child might be in for a more rewarding experience in a school that greets you this way: "Welcome to _____ School. Please stop by the main office. Thank you."

Of course, don't judge a school's welcome by the sign only. An even better indication is the treatment by office staff. If you stand at the counter for a long time before someone even notices you, let alone asks to help, pay attention this time to your rising blood pressure. If the office staff is officious without being helpful, if no one can answer simple questions or direct you to someone who can, try another school.

IS THE SCHOOL CLEAN AND IN GOOD REPAIR?

If the school is dirty and in need of minor repairs and replacements, good education may still be going on, but don't count on it. An unclean school in disrepair usually means someone—maybe a lot of someones—doesn't care about the school and the people in it. The people who don't care might include the community, a governing board, or the principal. Even the teachers and students may have given up on their environment and—worst of all—education.

ARE HALLWAYS AND RESTROOMS MARKED BY GRAFFITI?

Remember the school reporter who said he could judge the quality of a school by the quality of its restrooms. An exaggeration? Yes, but...Here, again we're talking about symbolism. In this case, the graffiti not only shows the lack of maintenance but also may be a sign that students are undisciplined and disrespectful. If much of the graffiti is obscene or excessively aggressive, the student body may be full of children who were weaned on Beavis and Butthead and Howard Stern rather than on Sesame Street and Mr. Rogers.

ARE PLAY AREAS SAFE AND WELL EQUIPPED?

Schools in cities and towns may be limited on outside playground space, but what exists should allow children to play in safety. For example, children chasing a ball should be prevented from running into a busy street. Equipment that raises children off the ground (e.g., swings and slides) should be imbedded in sand or another substance that will help cushion inevitable falls. Make sure that play, indoors and out, is properly supervised. If children are using equipment that could be dangerous when used incorrectly (e.g., a trampoline), observe whether they are instructed about safe operation.

Data you should collect

In addition to asking questions and observing, parents need to collect data. Listed below are some of the statistics you should ask of the school(s) you are evaluating. In some cases, you can compare statistics you obtain with state and national averages listed in Appendix C (public schools), or with data collected by agencies listed in Appendix D, which include sources of private school statistics.

Average daily attendance (ADA).

Classroom teacher:student ratio. This is different from staff:student ratio. If you ask for the latter figure, the school may include the librarian, counselor, therapists, and other professional staff who see only a few children at a time. The resulting figure could be misleading if what you want to know is how many students, on average, a classroom teacher is responsible for (akin to class size). The average classroom teacher:student ratio has been dropping across the country. It went from 1:28 in 1960 to 1:19 in 1990. Remember, however, that a competent, creative teacher, especially if assisted by aides, can cope effectively with more than 19 students.

Current expenditure per pupil in ADA.

Standardized test scores. Most educators suggest that parents evaluating a school collect test scores for a 3- or 5-year period. What you are looking for, of course, are good or bad trends. Suppose, for example, the school simply advises that the average student last year scored in the 60th percentile on a reading test. The score would mean more if you learned that 3 years ago the average student scored in the 45th percentile, or the 65th percentile. If you have difficulty understanding the manner in which the school reports scores (even with the help of our glossary), ask for a full explanation. Be wary if no one can provide such an explanation.

Students per computer used for instruction. We have already indicated some of the ways computers are now used for group and individual instruction. While computers are not indispensable to a quality education, a very high ratio might indicate that a school is not taking full advantage of the teacher/learning methods and materials available. No reliable national average is available for comparison, but you might be guided by the classroom teacher:student ratio. If the student:computer ratio is about the same or lower, the school probably is making good use of the technology.

Students per music and art specialists. If you are concerned about instruction in the arts, then you want to know if the school has specialists in those fields and what the ratio of students to specialists is. The national organizations in these two fields recommend one specialist for approximately 300 students, which is a desirable size for an elementary school.

Teacher experience. The average years of experience among teachers can tell you something about a school's educational and financial philosophies. For example, a school's governing body may want a majority of teachers with less than 10 years experience because it is looking for people with new ideas, trained in new technology, and theoretically having optimum energy. The school's governing body also may want younger teachers because they are on the lower rungs of the salary ladder. On the other hand, you and the school might prefer more experienced teachers because you feel they know the subject matter better and are more apt to command the attention and respect of students.

Teacher salaries. No reliable correlation between teacher salaries and teacher competence exists. However, a school that pays its teachers substantially less than surrounding schools is likely not to attract the best available teachers. Ask about the salary scale in addition to average salary. For example, the school that is trying to attract young teachers may offer an above-average starting salary and below-average salaries at the top. On the other hand, the school that is looking for most experience and advanced degrees will likely reverse the scale.

Workbook

We've provided you with lots of ammu-
nition, perhaps more than you thought
you wanted or needed. Now you have
to go into action. The workbook pages
are designed so you can conduct your
evaluations with all the information
and guidance at hand. For easy reference, the questions, observations, and
data are listed in the same order as
they were in the previous sections.

The workbook provides space for
three separate school evaluations. If
you expect to conduct more than three
evaluations, you are welcome to photocopy the workbook pages. First, enter
the name(s) of the school(s) you are
evaluating.

School 1 _____

School 2 _____

School 3 _____

ELEMENTARY SCHOOL: QUESTIONS: ANSWERS AND NOTES
WHAT DOES THE SCHOOL'S MISSION STATEMENT SAY?

Notes:

School 1 _____

_____

_____

School 2 _____

_____

_____

School 3 _____

_____

_____

HOW MANY PRINCIPALS HAS THE SCHOOL HAD IN THE PAST 15 YEARS?

Answers: **School 1** _____   **School 2** _____   **School 3** _____

Notes:

School 1 _____

_____

_____

School 2 _____

_____

_____

School 3 _____

_____

_____

IS SCHOOL-BASED MANAGEMENT PRACTICED?

Answers: **School 1:** Yes/No   **School 2:** Yes/No   **School 3:** Yes/No

Notes:

School 1 _____

_____

_____

_____

School 2 _____

_____

_____

_____

School 3 _____

_____

_____

_____

IS THE SCHOOL ENGAGED IN RESTRUCTURING?

Answers: **School 1:** Yes/No   **School 2:** Yes/No   **School 3:** Yes/No

Notes:

School 1 _____

_____

_____

_____

School 2 _____

_____

_____

_____

School 3 _____

_____

_____

_____

WHAT IS THE SCHOOL'S TEACHING PHILOSOPHY?

Notes:

School 1 _____

_____

_____

School 2 _____

_____

_____

School 3 _____

_____

_____

WHAT IS THE SCHOOL'S HOMEWORK POLICY?

Notes:

School 1 _____

_____

_____

_____

School 2 _____

_____

_____

_____

_____

School 3 _____

_____

_____

_____

WHAT IS THE POLICY ON PLACING HANDICAPPED AND GIFTED CHILDREN?

Notes:

School 1 _____

_____

_____

School 2 _____

_____

_____

_____

School 3 _____

_____

_____

_____

DOES THE SCHOOL OFFER HEAD START AND/OR CHAPTER-1 PROGRAMS?

Answers: **School 1:** Yes/No   **School 2:** Yes/No   **School 3:** Yes/No

Notes:

School 1 _____

_____

_____

_____

School 2 _____

_____

_____

_____

School 3 _____

_____

_____

_____

HAS THE SCHOOL DEVISED LEARNING OUTCOMES?

Answers: **School 1:** Yes/No   **School 2:** Yes/No   **School 3:** Yes/No

Notes:

School 1 _____

_____

_____

School 2 _____

_____

_____

School 3 _____

_____

_____

WHAT SPECIAL SERVICES DOES THE SCHOOL OFFER?

Notes:

School 1 _____

_____

_____

_____

School 2 _____

_____

_____

_____

School 3 _____

_____

_____

_____

WHAT IS THE SCHOOL'S POLICY REGARDING WHO MAY CONTACT YOUR CHILD DURING SCHOOL HOURS OR AFTER SCHOOL?

Notes:

School 1 _____

_____

_____

_____

School 2 _____

_____

_____

_____

School 3 _____

_____

_____

_____

WHAT ARE THE REQUIREMENTS FOR ADMISSION?

Notes:

School 1 _____

_____

_____

_____

School 2 _____

_____

_____

_____

School 3 _____

_____

_____

_____

WHAT ORIENTATION PROGRAM IS OFFERED PARENTS AND STUDENTS, AND WHEN IS IT SCHEDULED?

Notes:

School 1 _____

_____

_____

_____

School 2 _____

_____

_____

_____

School 3 _____

_____

_____

_____

WHAT SCHOLARSHIPS AND FINANCIAL AID ARE AVAILABLE?

Notes:

School 1 _____

_____

_____

School 2 _____

_____

_____

School 3 _____

_____

_____

WHAT KNOWLEDGE AND SKILLS SHOULD AN ELEMENTARY SCHOOL BE TEACHING?

Answers: Consult Appendix B.

Notes:

School 1 _____

_____

_____

_____

School 2 _____

_____

_____

_____

School 3 _____

_____

_____

_____

HOW IS CURRICULUM DECIDED?

Notes:

School 1 _____

_____

_____

_____

School 2 _____

_____

_____

_____

School 3 _____

_____

_____

_____

HOW OFTEN ARE CURRICULUM AND TEXTBOOKS REVIEWED AND UPDATED?

Answers: **School 1** _____   **School 2** _____   **School 3** _____

Notes:

School 1 _____

_____

_____

School 2 _____

_____

_____

School 3 _____

_____

_____

DOES THE READING PROGRAM BALANCE PHONICS AND WHOLE-LANGUAGE INSTRUCTION?

Answers: **School 1:** Yes/No   **School 2:** Yes/No   **School 3:** Yes/No

Notes:

School 1 _____

_____

_____

School 2 _____

_____

_____

School 3 _____

_____

_____

DOES THE SCHOOL HAVE A WELL-EQUIPPED AND WELL-USED LIBRARY/MEDIA CENTER?

Answers: **School 1:** Yes/No   **School 2:** Yes/No   **School 3:** Yes/No

Notes:

School 1 _____

_____

_____

_____

School 2 _____

_____

_____

_____

School 3 _____

_____

_____

_____

HOW ARE COMPUTERS USED FOR INSTRUCTION?

Notes:

School 1 _____

_____

_____

_____

School 2 _____

_____

_____

_____

School 3 _____

_____

_____

_____

DOES THE SCHOOL TEACH VALUES?

Answers: **School 1:** Yes/No   **School 2:** Yes/No   **School 3:** Yes/No

Notes:

School 1 _____

_____

_____

_____

School 2 _____

_____

_____

_____

School 3 _____

_____

_____

_____

WHAT IS THE SCHOOL'S DISCIPLINE POLICY?

Notes:

School 1 _____

_____

_____

_____

School 2 _____

_____

_____

_____

School 3 _____

_____

_____

_____

DOES THE SCHOOL BUDGET ALLOW FOR REGULAR CUSTODIAL AND MAINTENANCE SERVICES AND PROMPT REPAIRS?

Answers: **School 1:** Yes/No **School 2:** Yes/No **School 3:** Yes/No

Notes:

School 1 _____

_____

_____

School 2 _____

_____

_____

School 3 _____

_____

_____

TO WHAT DEGREE ARE SCHOOL, PARENTS, AND OTHER LAYPERSONS INVITED TO HELP DECIDE BUDGET, CURRICULUM, PERSONNEL, AND OTHER POLICIES?

Notes:

School 1 _____

_____

_____

_____

School 2 _____

_____

_____

_____

School 3 _____

_____

_____

_____

HOW WELL DOES THE SCHOOL COMMUNICATE WITH PARENTS/COMMUNITY THROUGH PUBLICATIONS AND THE MEDIA?

Notes:

School 1 _____

_____

_____

_____

School 2 _____

_____

_____

_____

School 3 _____

_____

_____

_____

IN WHAT OTHER WAYS DOES THE SCHOOL COMMUNICATE TO PARENTS/COMMUNITY?

Notes:

School 1 _____

_____

_____

_____

School 2 _____

_____

_____

_____

School 3 _____

_____

_____

_____

HOW OFTEN ARE PARENT/TEACHER CONFERENCES SCHEDULED?

Answers: **School 1** _____ **School 2** _____ **School 3** _____

Notes:

School 1 _____

_____

_____

School 2 _____

_____

_____

School 3 _____

_____

_____

IS IT POSSIBLE TO MEET WITH TEACHERS AT TIMES OTHER THAN SCHEDULED CONFERENCES?

Answers: **School 1:** Yes/No   **School 2:** Yes/No   **School 3:** Yes/No

Notes:

School 1 _____

_____

_____

School 2 _____

_____

_____

School 3 _____

_____

_____

CAN YOU OBSERVE YOUR CHILD'S CLASS IN SESSION?

Answers: **School 1:** Yes/No   **School 2:** Yes/No   **School 3:** Yes/No

Notes:

School 1 _____

_____

_____

_____

School 2 _____

_____

_____

_____

School 3 _____

_____

_____

_____

WHAT IS THE SCHOOL POLICY ON SECURITY?

Notes:

School 1 _____

_____

_____

_____

School 2 _____

_____

_____

_____

School 3 _____

_____

_____

_____

HOW ARE STUDENTS CLASSIFIED AS GIFTED?

Notes:

School 1 _____

_____

_____

_____

School 2 _____

_____

_____

_____

School 3 _____

_____

_____

_____

HOW ARE STUDENTS CLASSIFIED AS EMOTIONALLY DISTURBED OR LEARNING DISABLED?

Notes:

School 1 _____

_____

_____

School 2 _____

_____

_____

School 3 _____

_____

_____

DO STUDENTS HAVE THE RIGHT TO AVOID SOME CONTROVERSIAL CURRICULUM ON THE ONE HAND, BUT EMBRACE SOME CONTROVERSIAL OPINIONS OR GROUPS ON THE OTHER?

Answers: **School 1:** Yes/No   **School 2:** Yes/No   **School 3:** Yes/No

Notes:

School 1 _____

_____

_____

_____

School 2 _____

_____

_____

_____

School 3 _____

_____

_____

_____

WHAT IS THE SCHOOL'S PROGRAM FOR STAFF DEVELOPMENT AND CONTINUING EDUCATION FOR TEACHERS?

Notes:

School 1 _____

_____

_____

_____

School 2 _____

_____

_____

_____

School 3 _____

_____

_____

_____

ARE SUCH SUBJECTS AS MUSIC, ART, PHYSICAL EDUCATION, AND HEALTH TAUGHT BY SPECIALISTS?

Answers: **School 1:** Yes/No   **School 2:** Yes/No   **School 3:** Yes/No

Notes:

School 1 _____

_____

_____

School 2 _____

_____

_____

School 3 _____

_____

_____

DOES THE SCHOOL HAVE REGULAR ACCESS TO SUCH PROFESSIONALS AS LIBRARIAN, PSYCHOLOGIST, COUNSELOR, THERAPIST, AND NURSE?

Notes:

School 1 _____

_____

_____

_____

School 2 _____

_____

_____

_____

School 3 _____

_____

_____

_____

ARE THERE TEACHER AIDES?

Answers: **School 1:** Yes/No   **School 2:** Yes/No   **School 3:** Yes/No

Notes:

School 1 _____

_____

_____

School 2 _____

_____

_____

School 3 _____

_____

_____

WHAT TESTS ARE GIVEN, AND HOW ARE THE RESULTS USED?

Notes:

School 1 _____

_____

_____

_____

School 2 _____

_____

_____

_____

School 3 _____

_____

_____

_____

HOW ARE TEST RESULTS REPORTED TO PARENTS?

Notes:

School 1 _____

_____

_____

_____

School 2 _____

_____

_____

_____

School 3 _____

_____

_____

_____

WHAT IS THE TRANSPORTATION POLICY?

Notes:

School 1 _____

_____

_____

School 2 _____

_____

_____

School 3 _____

_____

_____

OBSERVATION: ANSWERS AND NOTES

DO STUDENTS SEEM TO BE ACTIVELY INVOLVED IN LEARNING?

Answers: **School 1:** Yes/No   **School 2:** Yes/No   **School 3:** Yes/No

Notes:

School 1 _____

_____

_____

_____

School 2 _____

_____

_____

_____

School 3 _____

_____

_____

_____

DO TEACHERS MANAGE THE CLASSROOM EFFECTIVELY?

Answers: **School 1:** Yes/No   **School 2:** Yes/No   **School 3:** Yes/No

Notes:

School 1 _____

_____

_____

_____

_____

School 2 _____

_____

_____

_____

_____

School 3 _____

_____

_____

_____

_____

IS STUDENTS' WORK PROMINENTLY DISPLAYED IN CLASSROOMS AND ON THE WALLS OF CORRIDORS?

Answers: **School 1:** Yes/No   **School 2:** Yes/No   **School 3:** Yes/No

Notes:

School 1 _____

_____

_____

School 2 _____

_____

_____

School 3 _____

_____

_____

ARE VISITORS, ESPECIALLY PARENTS, WARMLY WELCOMED?

Answers: **School 1:** Yes/No   **School 2:** Yes/No   **School 3:** Yes/No

Notes:

School 1 _____

_____

_____

_____

School 2 _____

_____

_____

_____

School 3 _____

_____

_____

_____

IS THE SCHOOL CLEAN AND IN GOOD REPAIR?

Answers: **School 1:** Yes/No   **School 2:** Yes/No   **School 3:** Yes/No

Notes:

School 1 _____

_____

_____

School 2 _____

_____

_____

School 3 _____

_____

_____

ARE HALLWAYS AND RESTROOMS MARKED BY GRAFITTI?

Answers: **School 1:** Yes/No   **School 2:** Yes/No   **School 3:** Yes/No

Notes:

School 1 _____

_____

_____

_____

School 2 _____

_____

_____

_____

School 3 _____

_____

_____

_____

ARE PLAY AREAS SAFE AND WELL-EQUIPPED?

Answers: **School 1:** Yes/No   **School 2:** Yes/No   **School 3:** Yes/No

Notes:

School 1 _____

_____

_____

School 2 _____

_____

School 3 _____

_____

_____

DATA: ANSWERS AND NOTES

DATA: AVERAGE DAILY ATTENDANCE (ADA)

Answers: School 1 _____ School 2 _____ School 3 _____

Notes:

School 1 _____

_____

_____

_____

School 2 _____

_____

_____

_____

School 3 _____

_____

_____

_____

DATA: CLASSROOM TEACHER:STUDENT RATIO

Answers: School 1 ____ : ____ School 2 ____ : ____ School 3 ____ : ____

Notes:

School 1 _____

_____

_____

School 2 _____

_____

_____

School 3 _____

_____

_____

DATA: CURRENT EXPENDITURES PER PUPIL IN ADA

Answers: **School 1** $_____   **School 2** $_____   **School 3** $_____

Notes:

School 1 _____

_____

School 2 _____

_____

School 3 _____

_____

DATA: STANDARDIZED ACHIEVEMENT TEST AVERAGE SCORES

Answers:

School 1:

Name of achievement test: _____

Reading: Year___ Score ___ / Year___ Score ___ / Year___ Score ___

Year___ Score ___ / Year___ Score ___ / Year___ Score ___

Math: Year___ Score ___ / Year___ Score ___ / Year___ Score ___

Year___ Score ___ / Year___ Score ___ / Year___ Score ___

Notes: _____

_____

_____

School 2:

Name of achievement test: _____

Reading: Year___ Score ___ / Year___ Score ___ / Year___ Score ___

Year___ Score ___ / Year___ Score ___ / Year___ Score ___

Math: Year___ Score ___ / Year___ Score ___ / Year___ Score ___

Year___ Score ___ / Year___ Score ___ / Year___ Score ___

Notes: _____

_____

_____

School 3:

Name of achievement test: _____

Reading: Year____ Score ____ / Year ____ Score ____ / Year ____ Score ____

Year ____ Score ____ / Year ____ Score ____ / Year ____ Score ____

Math: Year ____ Score ____ / Year ____ Score ____ / Year ____ Score ____

Year ____ Score ____ / Year ____ Score ____ / Year ____ Score ____

Notes: _____

_____

_____

DATA: STUDENTS PER COMPUTER USED FOR INSTRUCTION

Answers: **School 1** ____ : ____   **School 2** ____ : ____   **School 3** ____ : ____

Notes:

School 1 _____

_____

_____

_____

_____

School 2 _____

_____

_____

_____

_____

School 3 _____

_____

_____

_____

_____

DATA: STUDENTS PER MUSIC AND ART SPECIALISTS

Answers:

Music: **School 1** ____ : ____   **School 2** ____ : ____   **School 3** ____ : ____

Art: **School 1** ____ : ____   **School 2** ____ : ____   **School 3** ____ : ____

Notes:

School 1 _____

_____

_____

School 2 _____

_____

_____

School 3 _____

_____

_____

DATA: AVERAGE NUMBER OF YEARS OF TEACHER EXPERIENCE

Answers: **School 1** _____   **School 2** _____   **School 3** _____

Notes:

School 1 _____

_____

_____

School 2 _____

_____

_____

School 3 _____

_____

_____

DATA: AVERAGE TEACHER'S SALARY

Answers: **School 1** $\$$_____   **School 2** $\$$_____   **School 3** $\$$_____

Notes:

School 1 _____

_____

_____

_____

School 2 _____

_____

_____

_____

School 3 _____

_____

_____

_____

PART 4

Evaluating a Secondary School

T he *secondary school* is defined as grades 7 through 12 and includes what are commonly referred to as the *middle school* (occasionally in some locales still called a *junior high school*) and the *high school*.

As was true for Part 3, this part also is divided into five sections: (1) Parents, know your child; (2) Questions you should ask (3) Observations you should make; (4) Data you should collect; and (5) Workbook.

Parents, know your child

Once, when their older son was in middle school, his parents considered seeing a psychologist about his unusual behavior—until they discovered that every other boy his age behaved the same way. "Many of the contradictions, contrasts, and conflicts you see in your young teenager and preteenager are quite normal," reassured the authors of *The Middle School Years* (National Committee for Citizens in Education).

They identified these five common traits among young teenagers:

1. A high level of emotional and physical energy combined with long periods of "hanging out" and doing nothing productive by adult standards.
2. Indulging in risk-taking behavior, yet having feelings easily hurt.
3. A desire to be more independent from families and at the same time a need to be nurtured and protected.
4. Being self-absorbed and craving privacy, together with great concern about being accepted by the group.
5. Demanding privileges but avoiding responsibility, at the same time as developing a deep concern about social and other issues.

Of course, as middle school students move into high school, their hormones are still racing, and changes noted in the early teens often become even more pronounced in the late teens. But high-schoolers also are trying to be more adult like, so they may make an effort to limit erratic energy while forcing themselves to assume more responsibility for their life, present and future.

Recognition and acceptance become, if anything, a greater concern in high school. "Schools are places of strict boundaries, both physical and social," wrote Ernest L. Boyer in his book *High School*.

> Students are roughly divided into winners and losers. Such division may be in the classroom, where students compete with each other for the teacher's attention or praise, or through the grading system, or on the athletic field, or through acceptance or rejection by peers. Wherever it is, students quickly learn that they are in competition with each other. Many people call this phenomenon *peer pressure*.

All of the above describes your child in secondary school to a greater or lesser degree. It's that degree you have to be concerned about. You need to know how these traits and realities of the teenage years affect your child as a person and as a student. Here are some questions to ask yourself:

HOW IS OUR CHILD'S SELF-ESTEEM?

Perhaps, you already have heard more than you care to about self-esteem, but it is important. If you reexamine the forces shaping the teenager, you can see how someone's self-image at this stage could easily be damaged. For example: Your child is convinced that peers are more mature physically and emotionally—stronger, prettier. Your child is having trouble harnessing emotional energy and believes that "flaw" will lead to some dire consequence. Your child has been rejected by some peer group for no apparent reason and sees this as evidence of still other "flaws."

Telling a teenager to shake off a poor self-image will not help, of course. The problem may go away by itself in time, but before it does the teenager could be in serious trouble. The child may try to compensate for poor self-image by attracting attention through exaggerated behavior. Or the child might withdraw and give up, thus affecting both social life and academic performance.

If you believe your child suffers from especially low and persistent self-esteem, ask the school principal whether counseling or a support group is available to students with low self-esteem.

WHAT ARE YOUR CHILD'S GENUINE GIFTS, APTITUDES, AND INTERESTS?

In most families today, there is no inflexible expectation that children will follow in their parents' footsteps. However, that parental pressure of old has been replaced in many households by another pressure: Get a college degree! For one thing, these parents say that (and they are heavily reinforced by many school counselors) the degree is necessary for a good job and salary. Sometimes this advice (warning) to the secondary school student is made without any regard to what the student is best suited for or what the student wishes to accomplish in life. Furthermore, the part about good job and salary may be neither accurate nor realistic.

Everyone in education, business, and industry acknowledges that mastery of tomorrow's technology will be crucial. In fact, Dr. Boyer in his book recommended that *all* high school students take a one-semester course in technology: "not computer literacy but technology literacy." However, a number of post–high school institutions other than 4-year colleges exist that prepare students with above-average ability and interest for the thousands of highly skilled, highly paid, high-tech jobs that are even now opening up. Why, then, force students with that aptitude and desire into a college preparatory track?

Furthermore, a college degree is now an option at any stage of life. In fact, some of the better students in 4-year colleges today are those in their late 20s and 30s.

Of course, it is also possible to steer a student wrongly toward a vocational-technical track simply because the student, at least for the moment, seems lost in academic subjects or is at a particularly rebellious stage and it is thought that the voc-tech track will be more likely to relieve the student of academic anxiety or tame the rebelliousness.

Therefore, take stock of your child's real skills and reasonable plans and possibilities for the future, and be guided accordingly. Once a student is placed in a high school track, it may be difficult to switch.

HOW DOES YOUR CHILD RESPOND TO CHALLENGES AND STRESS?

According to the booklet *The Middle School Years,* "educators believe that the seeds for dropping out in high school are planted during the middle school years. In a government-funded survey...the characteristic most strongly associated with early school leaving is being behind in grade." Some students, faced with school challenges they are not equal to, decide that the only relief from the resulting stress is to get away from the challenges.

The challenge for some students may be tough courses for which they have not been properly prepared. Or, as stated above, they may be on a track that is not in synch with who and what they are. Some very bright and active students fail because they are overburdened by difficult courses, too many extracurricular activities, too active a social life, and/or an after-school or weekend job.

Some students may be unable to meet the challenge of a very large school (enrollment in the thousands) or large classes (30-plus students). They find it difficult to be noticed in class and have trouble making friends. They may need a smaller school where more individual help is available in classes and where friendships can bloom and not be smothered by the crowd.

Students face a myriad of other challenges and stresses in today's world: for example, absent parent(s) and easy access to drugs, alcohol, media violence, and sexual encounters beyond their emotional and intellectual maturity.

Pay attention to what your child says—and doesn't say—about challenges and stress. Be a careful observer and listener. If your child has been unusually irritable, uncommunicative, or lethargic, these could be signs that your child has not adapted to challenges and is under severe stress. Get help, and seek a school environment that doesn't add to the stress.

Questions you should ask

You probably will want to direct most of your questions to the school principal, but also remember to talk to teachers and other staff members, parents of students, and some students. Many of your questions may be asked at a school-sponsored orientation or by appointment, but don't pass up other opportunities. You should be able to talk briefly with teachers, other staff people, and students when you tour a school. However, you also may want to attend a meeting of the school's parent organization. And it might be helpful to ask questions of colleagues where you work, real estate salespeople, local shopkeepers and their customers, and an editor or education reporter for a local or regional newspaper.

Whereas you may be almost entirely responsible for deciding on an elementary school for your child, you may want to involve your child to a greater degree when evaluating a secondary school. Your child need not be present for all your questioning, observations, and data collection, but the child's "sense" of the school and its student body, as well as yours, is important.

Peter Bachmann, headmaster of the Flintridge Preparatory School (grades 7 to 12) in La Canada, California, said parents and students need to trust their intuition about a school. "They should have a good feeling about the school they are looking at," he said. It may be helpful for you and your child to make one tour of a school together. Your child, then, may also want to talk informally with students wherever they gather after school.

The questions and rationales that follow have been compiled from interviews with principals, parents, and representatives of major national education organizations, as well as from a number of books and articles written by educators and laypersons. Consult Appendix A for more information about sources. The questions are listed under 12 headings, from Administration/ Organization to Transportation.

ADMINISTRATION /ORGANIZATION

WHAT ARE THE SCHOOL'S GOALS?

Rationale: In his book *High School*, Ernest L. Boyer, one of America's foremost educators, wrote:

> When we asked teachers, principals, and students about school goals, their response frequently was one of uncertainty, amusement, or surprise. After visiting schools from coast to coast, we are left with the distinct impression that high schools lack a clear and vital mission.

Boyer and his researchers found that most state and local education goals, where they existed, were so vague as to be useless. He cited a number of bad examples of goal statements, including this one:

> The _____ School is vitally aware that the school of today is the school of the people it serves. The school provides educators who are knowledgeable in their subject matter and who are dedicated to serving all students and their needs.

You need to find out the goals—the mission—of the schools you are evaluating. In *High School,* Boyer provided a framework that you can use to judge a verbal or, preferably, written statement of goals or mission at the schools you are looking at. Here are Boyer's "essential goals." The high school should:

1. Help students develop the capacity to think critically and communicate effectively through a mastery of language.

2. Help all students learn about themselves, the human heritage, and the interdependent world in which they live through a core curriculum based on consequential human experiences common to all people.

3. Prepare all students for work and further education through a program of electives that develop individual aptitudes and interests.

4. Help all students fulfill their social and civic obligations through school and community service.

Principals caution parents to look carefully at goals and priorities and not to be afraid to question the principal closely about them. Headmaster Bachmann said parents should be wary of any school that doesn't have a set of well-defined goals or priorities. "If the principal can't tell you what the school's priorities are," he added, "maybe they don't have any."

The goals or mission statement of a public or private secondary school should indicate what the staff and governing body deem most important. Perhaps the school emphasizes study of the arts, or science, or communication skills. Maybe it stresses the importance of students' learning to obey strict discipline. The school may especially promote multiculturism or, as Boyer advocated, the school may put great stock in students' volunteering their service in the community.

Finally, not only question the principal about a goal or mission statement, but also ask the principal to describe briefly how the school strives to meet the goals or carry out its mission. "You need to weigh what is against what is supposed to be," advised John A. Lammel, director of high school services for the National Association of Secondary School Principals.

IS THE SCHOOL ENGAGED IN STRATEGIC PLANNING?

Rationale: Planning should be closely tied to goals or mission. For example, the school may have a long-range plan for increasing the uses of technology in the classroom. Or it may be planning over several years to reduce class size in core subject areas, thereby also requiring the school to look ahead at staffing and budget needs.

WHAT IS THE POLICY ON TRACKING AND PLACEMENT?

Rationale: Although some public and many private schools offer only a college-preparatory track, most public schools have three tracks: general studies, college preparatory, and vocational-technical. Students are often placed a particular track, at least by the end of middle school. Once placed, it may be difficult for a student to change tracks.

What you first want to know are the bases for placement. These may include teacher recommendations, test scores, and results of aptitude tests. Next, ask about the flexibility of the tracking system. May a student move from one track to another? Does it ever happen? If a school boasts of great flexibility, be cautious and probe further. Some schools have done some students a great disservice by switching them from general studies or vocational-technical to college preparatory so late that they graduate from high school without having taken all the courses they need to succeed in college.

WHAT IS THE POLICY ON ABILITY GROUPING?

Rationale: As in the case of tracking, once a student is grouped according to ability, it may be difficult to be reassigned even when the student seems to demonstrate greater ability. For example, a student may be placed on the college-preparatory track but assigned to low-ability classes in all major subjects. Again, find out how students are assigned an ability level and under what circumstances they can move from one level to another.

DOES THE SCHOOL PRACTICE SCHOOL-BASED MANAGEMENT?

Rationale: School-based management is defined in the glossary (Part 2) and also discussed in Part 3. What you want to learn is whether such a practice is fully or partially employed, or if it is not used at all. If school-based management is practiced in whole or in part, ask the principal and some teachers and parents how it is working.

WHAT IS THE ATTENDANCE POLICY?

Rationale: Many high schools that adopted open campus policies in the 70s have changed their minds. Too many students drifted away after homeroom or at lunch time. You should ask if attendance is kept not only by homeroom teachers but by other teachers as well. Are parents called when students are frequently absent? You also may want to ask the public school whether it employs truant officers or asks local police to crack down on chronic absentees.

WHAT IS THE HOMEWORK POLICY?

Rationale: If there is no policy, it may indicate that the school attaches little importance to students' study outside the classroom. The policy does not have to dictate a certain number of hours of homework per day or week, but it should indicate that the school expects teachers to assign homework and expects students to complete the assignments promptly. The amount, nature, and frequency of homework may vary from subject to subject. The policy should say what the value of homework is. For example: It reinforces learning that begins in the classroom; it may help slower students catch up with their peers and enable brighter students to move ahead with more challenging material; it also prepares students for the demands of college.

HOW MANY PRINCIPALS (HEADMASTERS) HAS THE SCHOOL HAD IN THE PAST 15 YEARS?

Rationale: Frequent turnover among top school administrators generally signals trouble. Usually, it means one of two things: (1) The governing body either has poorly screened candidates or chosen unwisely; (2) there are deep-seated problems regarding teachers teaching and/or students learning.

HOW MANY ADMINISTRATORS ARE THERE, AND WHAT ARE THEIR DUTIES?

Rationale: The number of administrators and their duties are dictated in part by the size and organization of the school. A rule of thumb is that a secondary school adds an assistant principal for approximately every 200 students over 500. A school with an enrollment of 1,000, for example, will likely have two or three assistant principals.

One question to ask is whether the administrators see themselves primarily as instructional leaders rather than as people merely responsible for running the school in an orderly fashion. A principal is quoted in *High School Leaders and Their Schools* (National Association of Secondary School Principals) as stating:

Instruction is the most important thing in the school. All that we do in this school is done to support instruction. Any new programs that we implement, purchases we make, disciplinary actions, or even field trips students take are all done in the interest of improving instruction.

A school can be top-heavy with administrators. A clue to this problem is an unusually large number of middle managers, a layer of administrators between assistant principals, for example, and department chairs. If this situation exists in a school you are evaluating, ask about these managers' specific duties and how they were appointed. In some schools, teachers who have lost their effectiveness (or never had it) but are tenured are kicked upstairs. The Peter Principle may apply; that is, they are even less effective on the top rungs of the ladder than they were below.

ADMISSIONS

WHAT ARE THE REQUIREMENTS FOR ADMISSION?

Rationale: Admission to a public secondary school is almost automatic if the student has satisfactorily completed elementary school, except in certain circumstances. These may include the following: admission into special schools (e.g., gifted) or magnet schools, admission into a school outside the district where the student lives, and admission into a school where the student body must be racially balanced because of court order or district policy.

Admission to a private school may be subject to other criteria, including the number of available spaces and demonstrated achievement in the lower grades, as opposed to simply having completed them. A private school may require the student to pass certain tests or otherwise prove mastery of basic skills in reading, writing, and computation. Furthermore, the private school may be looking for students with special talents or those who meet a certain demographic profile. For example, the school may want more students with talent in the arts in addition to academic ability. Or perhaps the school wants to increase the number of minority students or girls or students from middle-income families.

WHAT KIND OF ORIENTATION IS OFFERED STUDENTS AND PARENTS?

Rationale: At the elementary level, orientation is probably more important for the parent than the child. The reverse may be true at the secondary level. The student has to make some major adjustments—for example: exposure to more subjects and more freedom to choose courses, working out a class schedule and moving from room to room and teacher to teacher, selecting from among many cocurricular activities, and meeting many strangers among the larger student body and making new friends.

Therefore, find out about the orientation for students as well as for parents. In most public school districts, orientation to the middle school takes place during the last year of elementary school, and orientation to high school is offered during the last year of middle school. Additional student orientation may take place at the start of middle school and high school. (See the category *Students.*)

WHAT SCHOLARSHIPS OR OTHER FINANCIAL AID ARE AVAILABLE?

Rationale: Tuition at private (including parochial) schools can be expensive. If you are looking for a boarding school, then, of course, there are additional charges. Some private schools have both an admissions officer and a financial aid officer. At other institutions, the position may be combined. Inquire about the full range of possibilities. Some sources of aid are as follows: the school itself, alumni and parents' groups, organizations and associations, government agencies, small foundations, and religious and fraternal institutions. Aid may be in the form of scholarships, grants, or loans.

A booklet that may be helpful is titled *Financial Options* and is available from the National Association of Independent Schools (NAIS), 1800 M Street, Suite 460 South, Washington, DC 20036.

CURRICULUM

WHAT KNOWLEDGE AND SKILLS SHOULD A STUDENT IN SECONDARY SCHOOL BE LEARNING?

Rationale: National standards in many subjects have been drafted and should be available through the school you are evaluating or from the U.S. Department of Education (see Appendix C). These standards and the general frameworks adopted by the National Assessment of Educational Progress (Appendix B) are guides as to what *all* students should have learned.

Twelve years ago, the College Board (the same organization that administers the Scholastic Achievement Test) published a booklet titled *Academic*

Preparation for College: What students need to know and be able to do. The booklet was written from the suggestions of hundreds of school and college teachers. It is still available and is still most helpful. The booklet lists, for example, basic academic competencies a student should have mastered before graduation from high school. One of the dozens of competencies included is this one under the subject of writing: "The ability to gather information from primary and secondary sources; to write a report using this research; to quote, paraphrase, and summarize accurately; and to cite sources properly."

It is my unfortunate duty as an instructor of writing at a state college to advise you that few college sophomores and fewer freshmen have this ability. Many—too many—freshmen claim they had no writing course in high school and wrote nothing more than book reports or what we call *cut-and-paste papers* that include huge blocks of material taken directly from sources but showing very little paraphrase or summary. Using this booklet as a guide (see Appendix C for more information), you should be able to question principals and department chairpersons about aspects of the curriculum. For example, are the research/writing skills mentioned above taught by the school you are evaluating? If so, when are they taught? And it wouldn't be a bad idea to ask to see some recent student research reports (without names).

HOW IS CURRICULUM DECIDED?

Rationale: For public secondary schools, most states mandate that schools offer so many years or Carnegie units in the major subjects. However, a number of states more directly influence the secondary school curriculum through a statewide basic skills or competency test (see glossary, Part 2) that students must pass prior to graduation. Graduation requirements are decided by the school board, but specific learning outcomes are usually developed primarily by teachers, department chairs, and other administrators. Parents also may be involved, particularly in schools where school-based management is practiced.

Of course, at private schools, teachers play an even greater role in devising curriculum. At schools affiliated with a church or religious denomination, some aspects of the curriculum may be determined by religious authorities.

At any school you are evaluating, ask to see curriculum guides for subjects of particular interest to you. Be wary of a school that cannot show you such guides.

WHAT ELECTIVES ARE OFFERED, AND IS CHOICE CONTROLLED?

Rationale: The excesses of the 70s, when some students breezed through high school by selecting a number of "soft" electives, are mostly at an end. However, you should carefully examine elective courses and ask what guidance is offered students when choosing electives.

According to today's leading education reformers, many secondary schools now require *all* students to select courses from a core curriculum that includes the major academic subjects. The selection of electives is limited, and many are directly related to the core subjects. Now, instead of having course options such as Poetry Through Rock and Roll or History of Sports, students may choose Modern American Poets or History of Non-Western Cultures.

If the school you are looking at still offers a very broad spectrum of electives, many of which are only vaguely related to a core curriculum, and if students receive little guidance in choosing from among the smorgasbord, that school may still be operating under the curse of the 70s. The school may not be for your child of the 90s or 21st century.

IS THE VOCATIONAL-TECHNICAL CURRICULUM CURRENT?

Rationale: Whether the voc-tech curriculum is offered by a comprehensive high school or a regional school, it should be up-to-date. It should be preparing students for existing or future careers, using the techniques and equipment of those careers. For example, if printing is taught but the school has no equipment with which to teach desktop publishing, the instruction is dated. If auto mechanics is taught but the school lacks the modern equipment that diagnoses engine problems, it is not current.

HOW OFTEN ARE CURRICULUM AND TEXTBOOKS REVIEWED?

Rationale: Someone has said that perhaps the greatest threat to education is the status quo. Knowledge is not static. Imagine studying the history of Europe using materials that are more than 5 years old. Nearly everything important has changed, from politics and economics to the map itself.

Most educators recommend curriculum and textbook review at least every 5 years, especially in mathematics and the social and physical sciences. Other resources also should be updated.

WHAT IS THE CURRICULUM IN THE ARTS?

Rationale: Most educators agree that the study of the arts is an integral part of a quality secondary school education. Ideally, courses should be offered in art, dance, music, and theater.

HOW ARE COMPUTERS USED FOR INSTRUCTION?

Rationale: The number of resources and the amount of information stored in computers have been expanding at an astonishing rate. Therefore, the computer has become a key tool in research for every subject. Also, the computer is increasingly used for the writing (and editing) of essays and the solving of mathematical and scientific problems. Students should have easy access to computers and a wide range of software. This means that computers should be available in classrooms, a computer lab (primarily for advanced instruction in computer use and programming), and the school library.

It is important to ask the principal, teachers, and students about computer usage. The mere presence of the hardware is not necessarily a guarantee that the machines are used wisely.

IS THE LIBRARY WELL STOCKED AND WELL EQUIPPED?

Rationale: Until recently, the American Library Association had a standard of 8,000 to 12,000 books (hard cover and paperback) for a high school library. While the organization still believes in standards, it prefers now to emphasize the importance of stocking a secondary school library with a sufficient and wide variety of print, visual, and audio materials that meet the curriculum goals of the school. Today, this means providing access to Internet or other computer network. Also, the library should have adequate space for shelving books and storing other materials, comfortable reading areas, and carrels for study and viewing of microfilm and microfiche.

DOES THE CURRICULUM REFLECT MULTICULTURISM?

Rationale: Multiculturism should not be a concept only talked about, nor should it be the title of an elective course. Literature courses should include authors of many nations and cultures, and American and world history courses should recount the participation of people of many backgrounds and colors and both sexes. For example, students should learn about the works of African-American writers in a survey course taken by all students; it should not be necessary to take an elective in black literature. Also, all students should know about the contributions made to the nation by women, Native Americans, African-Americans, and all other hyphenated Americans. They should not be made to learn these things in electives.

IS THERE INTERDISCIPLINARY INSTRUCTION?

Rationale: In some schools, teams of teachers representing different disciplines (subjects) work together on a joint theme. For example, a team composed of teachers of science, history, and English

might devise a course pertaining to environmental problems. The science teacher could help students study physical conditions; the history teacher could assist students in tracing the development of environmental problems and solutions through the decades; and the English teacher could assign essays based on students' research and reasoning.

The key questions to ask about such courses are these: (1) How important and well conceived is the theme? (2) Are learning materials adequate and current? (3) Is each teacher effective?

IS COURSE SCHEDULING FLEXIBLE?

Rationale: A recent report by the National Education Commission on Time and Learning was critical of secondary schools that schedule all classes for the same amount of time (51 minutes on average). Schools should schedule longer blocks of time for core academic subjects, for example, stated the commission. If you are concerned that your child spend most of his or her time on core academic subjects, ask about block or modular scheduling that achieves that end.

You also should check whether your child will be able to get the courses that may be needed to fulfill plans for college and career. For example, your child may need an advanced math or science course for admission to a college major. However, because of the small size of the student body there may not be enough students to warrant a section of that course. Perhaps there are just enough students for one section taught during one period only. But your child needs another top-level course, which, because of the small number of students, is also scheduled for one period only. Guess what? The courses are scheduled for the same hour. In larger schools, with more students and teachers, it is often possible to schedule more than one section of an advanced course.

DOES THE HIGH SCHOOL OFFER ADVANCED PLACEMENT COURSES?

Rationale: The Advanced Placement (AP) Program is sponsored by the College Board. Qualified students (those with high ability) may enroll in one or more college-level courses, primarily in academic subjects and the arts. If they do well in the courses, they may receive credit from the college of their choice, and, therefore, they need not take the equivalent courses in college. High school teachers of AP courses usually are among the most effective teachers on the faculty, and they receive additional training as instructors in the AP Program.

DISCIPLINE

WHAT IS THE SCHOOL'S DISCIPLINE POLICY?

Rationale: A discipline policy should be written, and it should be made available to parents and students (e.g., in a handbook). It is important that you and your child know what specific behavior or actions are subject to some form of punishment and whether punishments are scaled according to severity and frequency of the infraction. The discipline policy also should describe an appeal process. In most states, students in public schools may appeal suspension and expulsion (see the Discipline category

in Part 2). Recently, some schools have taken very tough stances on student fights and other major disturbances. They immediately turn student troublemakers over to local police for prosecution.

It is especially important to check the discipline policy at a private school, since it is usually not subject to the restrictions and guidelines established by state authorities for public schools. For example, the handbook for a private school affiliated with a church states that the "normal order for discipline will include demerit, detention, spanking, probation, suspension, and expulsion." The policy also states that three demerits mean 20 minutes of detention, four demerits mean 30 minutes, and so on. What the policy never states, however, are the grounds for giving demerits and how many detention minutes lead to spanking, probation, etc. The school does have a dress code, and male students' hair must be "neatly trimmed and combed." However, students and parents are left to wonder whether demerits are given boys whose hair does not conform and, if so, how many demerits (one for each 16th of an inch of hair over the ear?).

In its book *The Middle School Years,* the National Committee for Citizens in Education warns: "Suspension from school has become a widely used form of discipline," and "many school administrators suspend students for skipping school, using foul language, or making a mess in the lunchroom." Therefore, you are advised to ask school authorities to explain fully any vague or

missing language referring to infractions and punishments.

MAINTENANCE

DOES THE SCHOOL HAVE AN EFFEC-
TIVE POLICY FOR ONGOING
MAINTENANCE AND REPAIR AND
LONG-TERM RENOVATION?

Rationale: "More than 50% of the [pub-
lic] schools in use today were built
during the 1950s and 1960s, generally
a time of rapid and cheap construction,"
stated the Education Writers Association
in its report on the condition of public
schools in America titled *Wolves at the
Schoolhouse Door.*

> These mid-century buildings are
> wearing out quickly and have severe
> repair needs. . . . Many construction
> experts say the buildings were
> intended to last only about 30 years.
> If so, their time is up.

Although the EWA study did not
include private schools, much of what
it reported about public schools applies
to many private school buildings as
well. Of course, maintenance and
repairs at a public, middle, and high
school, particularly long-range planning for major projects, are usually
part of a districtwide policy covering
a number of buildings and subject to
the approval of a central board and
administration. On the other hand, an
independent private school (as opposed,
for example, to a Roman Catholic high
school that is part of a diocese) has more
direct control over maintenance/ repair
policies and planning.

You should ask school authorities
about the age of the school building,
their policy for regular maintenance,
and their plans for making major repairs
and renovations.

PARENTS/COMMUNITY
INVOLVEMENT

HOW ACTIVE ARE THE PARENTS
OF STUDENTS?

Rationale: "A major factor in problem
schools is the parents," says Ronald
Ganschinietz, principal of the senior high
school in Collinsville, Illinois (enrollment: 2,000 in grades 9 to 12). "In those
schools, the parents' organization tends
to be small and weak. It should be just
the reverse." Many educators talk about
the drastic decline in parental involvement that occurs when the children
leave elementary school and enter secondary school.

These observers offer two related
explanations for the phenomenon. First,
they say, parents of teenagers believe
their children are better able to chart
their own education once they have theoretically mastered the basics in
elementary school and matured. Second,
parents are turned away by their children, who are convinced they can do it
all on their own. Both statements are
unrealistic. Of course, parents sometimes complain that their questions and
comments are not welcomed by school
administrators and teachers.

Whatever the reasons for the drop
in parental involvement, it is not
healthy for the parents, their children,
or the school. Therefore, ask questions
about the school's organization for parents: level of parent participation, how
often the group meets, and what its purpose and goals are, what have been its
accomplishments in recent months and

years. Ask the principal how the school administration and faculty involve parents in making important decisions. Don't be satisfied with vague statements such as "we always welcome parent participation in decision making." If there is no clear-cut, written policy to follow, chances are nothing much is happening.

HOW ACCESSIBLE TO PARENTS ARE THE TEACHERS?

Rationale: In elementary school, where students spend most of their day with one teacher, it is fairly simple to arrange one-on-one meetings between teachers and parents at least twice a year. It isn't so easy at the secondary school, where students may have classes with as many as a half-dozen teachers. However, this problem should not prevent private meetings between parents and teachers. Ask what procedure the school has for parent-teacher conferences (usually held near the end of grading periods). The policy may require you to make a separate appointment with each teacher and to plan in advance of the meetings what questions you want to ask of your child's teachers. Also, ask whether you can bring your child to such meetings, if that is what you want to do (a good idea in many instances).

DOES THE SCHOOL'S GOVERNING BOARD AND ADMINISTRATION REGULARLY INFORM PARENTS AND THE COMMUNITY ABOUT SCHOOL POLICIES, PROGRAMS, AND ACTIVITIES?

Rationale: Every secondary school, public or private, has its community in addition to parents of students. For the public school, it includes citizen-tax-payers, local business and civic leaders, and local government officials. For the private school, community may include alumni, former faculty members and trustees, benefactors, and other friends of the school.

You will want to know how the school communicates with these audiences. You might want to ask about (and look at) a school newsletter (published at least four times a year), an annual report, and special project and planning reports. Also, does the school report on important developments to the news media serving the parents and larger community, and does the school encourage media coverage of activities other than sports?

CAN YOU OBSERVE CLASSES IN SESSION?

Rationale: Most teachers do not like to be interrupted if they are in the midst of lecturing or giving instructions. However, they may welcome visitors when students are working on their own or in small groups. Ask the principal what the school's policy is, because it is in your and your child's interest to observe different teaching and learning styles. (See also Section 3.)

SECURITY

WHAT IS THE SCHOOL POLICY ON SECURITY?

Rationale: The first thing to ask about is how the school controls visitors. Are doors other than the main entrance locked to outsiders but open for students exiting (see also Section 3)? Are hallways monitored by people or video cameras? In most schools, some monitoring of halls and restrooms is conducted regularly by students, faculty on break time, administrators, or volunteer parents.

Also ask about searches of restrooms and students' lockers and cars (perhaps also students' rooms at a boarding school). Are such searches conducted on some regular basis or only when there is probable cause to suspect that a student is hiding illegal weapons or drugs? In either situation, you may want to ask about the results of such searches. Don't be afraid to ask direct questions about the number of cases when drugs (including alcohol) or weapons have been found.

STUDENTS

WHAT COCURRICULAR ACTIVITIES ARE AVAILABLE TO STUDENTS?

Rationale: Students should have opportunities to be elected to an active student government and to join sports teams, organizations connected to academic subjects (e.g., French club), and organizations related to personal interests (e.g., student newspaper). Ask whether such activities are mostly scheduled during the regular school day or after hours. Also, inquire about fees.

In recent years, an increasing number of public and private schools have offered students the chance to engage in community service. In some schools, community service may be required for graduation. For example, the state of Maryland mandates community service for all students prior to graduation. Students may receive academic credit for their service. Typically, community service is performed in child or senior day care centers, hospitals, nursing homes, senior residence facilities, homeless shelters, community or school libraries, fire departments, emergency squads, and other civic organizations. Tutoring other students or assisting a teacher may also fulfill a service requirement.

Most community service work is performed after school, on weekends, or during vacation periods.

ARE VERY BRIGHT STUDENTS CHALLENGED?

Rationale: We already have mentioned the Advanced Placement Program, but you also might ask about honors classes, independent study, and study/travel abroad. Ask to see the descriptions of such programs and talk to teachers, parents, and students involved in them. These programs can differ markedly from school to school. Honors classes and independent study at some places simply mean students are left to their own devices without much guidance, stimulation, monitoring, or accountability. Even gifted students need a wise mentor to help them select a topic for special study and to be available as a resource and guide.

Another program worth asking about is International Baccalaureate. The program offers in-depth study over an extended period. Students take three special courses for 2 years each and three courses for 1 year each.

Some public school districts and states sponsor separate schools for the gifted. In some cases they may be magnet schools limited to students who are very able in a special area, such as science or the arts. However, check out magnet schools carefully. The school may cater to any student with an interest in a special area, as opposed to only students with exceptional ability.

IN A LARGE SCHOOL, WHAT HAS BEEN DONE TO PREVENT STUDENTS FROM BECOMING "LOST" IN THE CROWD?

Rationale: It is easy for many young people to feel adrift with no safe harbor in a sea of 1,000, 2,000, or 3,000 students. Your child may be one of those young persons. A number of larger schools have recognized the problem and done something about it. Some arrangements you may want to ask about are these:

1. The large school is subdivided into smaller schools or *houses* (a term borrowed from private education), either within the same building or interconnected buildings. Each division has its own principal or headmaster and operates almost as a separate institution (which it is not).
2. Each teacher is assigned a small group of students for whom the teacher serves as mentor, adviser, listener, problem-solver, and, if necessary, a shoulder to cry on. Do not confuse this teacher with a homeroom teacher who sees a group of students for a few minutes at the start of the day and whose main task is taking attendance and giving the "instructions de jour." Nor is this person a guidance counselor who meets briefly with students once or twice a year to plan next year's schedule.

TEACHERS

IS THERE BALANCE AMONG THE FACULTY?

Rationale: The secondary school faculty should be balanced in several ways:

1. *Experience.* The faculty should include a good mix of teachers who have been performing well for a number of years and relatively new teachers (less than 10 years experience) who may contribute new ideas and new energy. The number of degrees earned is less important than a record of effective teaching.
2. *Sex.* Women should be well represented, and not just as teachers of business courses and girls' sports.
3. *Culture and race.* The world in which students live is peopled with persons of different cultures, ethnic backgrounds, and colors. This world should be represented on the faculty, but not to satisfy outside pressure or quotas.

DOES THE SCHOOL HAVE A STRONG, ONGOING TEACHER DEVELOPMENT PROGRAM?

Rationale: Ask for specifics. What on-campus and off-campus seminars, workshops, or courses have teachers attended in the last year or two that were designed to update them on new research and new techniques? If only a few teachers can attend such programs, are they then called upon to pass on what they have learned to other teachers? Does the school identify master teachers who are responsible for assisting teachers who may be having trouble adapting to new teaching methods and curriculum?

ARE TEACHERS PREPARED AND ENCOURAGED TO PRACTICE DIFFERENT TEACHING STYLES AND LEARNING METHODS?

Rationale: Lecturing (passive learning) should not be the only teaching style in use. Teachers also should be offering their students frequent opportunities for active learning: class discussion, working in small groups, and independent study. In addition, teachers should be making good use of a variety of teaching/learning materials. These should include printed materials other than textbooks and the audio and visual materials available on computers, television monitors, and other tools (see Curriculum; also see Section 3, this part).

DOES THE SCHOOL HAVE ENOUGH COUNSELORS AND OTHER SPECIALISTS?

Rationale: The American School Counselor Association recommends one counselor for every 250 to 350 students in middle school and one for every 200 to 300 students in high school. If the ratio is considerably more in the schools you are examining, it may mean that students are not receiving adequate guidance in post–high school preparation. Colleges and trade schools regularly report they receive many freshmen who have not taken all the courses they need to succeed after high school.

The secondary school also should have specialists who can help students with serious learning, emotional, and health problems.

ARE TEACHER AIDES USED?

Rationale: Teacher aides can free the teacher from paperwork, but, if properly trained, they also can monitor and provide direction for small- group work. In addition, aides can ready computers and other equipment for use by teacher and students and go to the library or media center to obtain materials. Finally, aides can help maintain order as necessary.

TESTING

DOES THE SCHOOL PRACTICE AUTHENTIC ASSESSMENT?

Rationale: Many educators advocate authentic assessment in addition to or in place of tests that measure students' achievement by how well they answer questions about specific knowledge and skills. Authentic assessment (see glossary, Part 2) measures students' learning by how well they can demonstrate their knowledge and skills.

For example, a student's progress in expository writing would be noted by examining the essays in the student's portfolio. The portfolio might follow the student through middle and high schools. Instead of only answering questions about the Civil War period in American history, a student might be asked to give an oral report based on independent research, as well as on what was learned in class.

If school officials say they practice authentic assessment, ask for specific examples. You then may want to talk to teachers who have worked with this form of testing. Do they believe this kind of assessment provides enough information about how well students have learned what they are supposed to?

HOW DO TEACHERS USE TEST RESULTS?

Rationale: Tests are designed to show whether students have learned what was taught to them (or what they have learned on their own from other sources). Therefore, the tests are valuable only if teachers and administrators use the test scores or assessment results to help students learn. The information should be used in these ways:

1. In the event of poor performance, a student might be assigned a tutor, given additional instruction in specific skills or knowledge, or moved to another class where the work is less demanding.

2. In the event of outstanding performance, a student might be encouraged to go beyond classwork through independent study, be moved to an honors class, or encouraged to take an Advanced Placement course.

HOW ARE TEST RESULTS REPORTED TO STUDENTS AND PARENTS?

Rationale: Ask to see examples of materials used by the school to report and interpret test data for students and parents. Such materials should include full explanations written in laypersons' language.

TRANSPORTATION

WHAT IS THE TRANSPORTATION POLICY?

Rationale: You should look for information about eligibility, scheduling, behavior, and discipline. For example, ask whether your child is eligible to be bused from near your home to the public or private school of your choice. The answer depends on state law and established bus routes. Also, if your child is eligible, what time does the bus pick up and drop off? Some parents change schools when they find out their child has to be at the bus stop by 6 o'clock in the morning. Also, if your child plans on after-school activities (e.g., sports, clubs, and community service), is there a late bus, or will other arrangements have to be made?

A good transportation policy will include rules for behavior on the bus and penalties for misbehavior. In some cases, students and parents have been surprised to learn that what they thought were minor infractions could be penalized by suspension.

Observations you should make

ARE STUDENTS ACTIVELY ENGAGED IN LEARNING?

As you walk the halls and look into classrooms, you should hear the noise of learning. And it should not be restricted to the drone of lecturing. Some students should be questioning the teacher; some should be working and discussing in small groups; some should be conducting experiments or solving problems; some might be reporting orally to the class; and others might be working alone at a computer. When you go by the library/media center, students should be working alone and in small groups.

ARE STUDENTS ROAMING THE HALLS DURING CLASSES?

If a number of students are roaming the halls when classes are in session, be concerned. It usually means one of two things: What is going on in the classrooms is not of interest, or teachers and administrators are lax in discipline. Of course, it could mean both things.

ARE STUDENTS' WORK AND AWARDS DISPLAYED PROMINENTLY?

You should see more than sports trophies. For example, awards for academic competition and students' art should be shown. Perhaps a showcase displays exceptional science projects. A plaque might cite the school and specific students for community service. What is mostly on display may indicate what the school values most.

IS THE SCHOOL CLEAN AND WELL MAINTAINED?

If floors are dirty and walls contain grafitti, they may be telling you that neither the administration, teachers, nor students have much respect for each other, for the building, and for learning. Look into restrooms. Sometimes, vandalism not apparent in the halls is revealed in the rest rooms. Look into classrooms. Are they well lighted and ventilated? Are windows and shades in good repair?

IS THE SCHOOL SECURE FROM UNAUTHORIZED VISITORS?

Signs should welcome visitors but direct them to the main office. If people aimlessly walking the halls appear to be slightly older than most students and show no pass, they may be outsiders who have no business being there.

ARE THERE ADEQUATE AND UP-TO-DATE MATERIALS AND EQUIPMENT?

As you inspect classrooms, library, vocational/technical shops, and physical education spaces, note such things as the following: the age and condition of books; whether computers, microfilm viewers, and other machinery are working; whether enough equipment exists to allow all members of a physical education class to be involved in some activity; and whether spaces are too small for the amount of equipment and/or the number of students.

Data you should collect

Your evaluation of a school is not complete without certain statistics. Educators suggest that you collect data for a 3- to 5-year period so comparisons can be made. For example, an average SAT score of 896 for 1984 might still be higher than the state average, but perhaps it is 10 points below what it was 3 years ago. In some cases you can compare local data with state and national statistics for public schools stated below or listed in Appendix C, or with data collected by other agencies listed in Appendix D.

Average daily attendance (ADA).

Classroom teacher:student ratio. In middle and high schools, class size can vary greatly. A class for students at the highest level of math, for example, is likely to be much smaller than a class in freshman English. However, the national average is approximately 1:15.

Competency test performance. Most states require students to pass a competency test of certain academic skills prior to graduation. The statistics to get are the percentages of students who pass the test at various grade levels and then, finally, pass in time for graduation.

Counselor:student ratio. The national standard set by the American School Counselors Association is 1:250–350 in middle school and 1:200–300 for high school.

Current expenditure per pupil.

Dropout rate. Schools may figure this rate differently, which makes it sometimes difficult to compare to other schools or to a state or national average. However, whatever a school's system for computing the dropout rate, it is still useful to compare the statistic over a 5-year period.

Graduation rate. This figure may be the same or similar to the dropout rate. It refers to the percentage of students who entered high school as freshmen and graduated 4 years later. It should be above 90 percent.

Graduates who go on to higher education. You may want to have this figure broken down as follows: percentage of students attending 4-year colleges, 2-year colleges, and technical schools. You also may want to ask whether the school conducts follow-up studies of graduates. If so, ask to see them.

Students per computer used for instruction. This figure should not be much higher than classroom teacher:student ratio.

Students taking the American College Testing Program's Assessment (ACT) or the Scholastic Achievement Test (SAT). The ACT is the test preferred by schools and colleges in many midwestern and southern states. It is an important statistic, especially when comparing ACT and SAT scores. For example, if only a small percentage of students took either test, the average score would likely be much higher than if a greater number of students took the test. A low percentage of students usually means that only the brightest ones took the test.

Students' average combined score on the ACT or SAT. A perfect combined SAT score (verbal and math) would be 1,000. Fewer schools and colleges consider these scores to be accurate reflectors of ability or predictors of performance in college.

Students enrolled in Advanced Placement courses and number of AP courses offered (more than 25 are available).

Students earning awards and honors. You may want to check these statistics: number of National Merit Scholarship finalists and semifinalists; how often academic teams (debating, science, etc.) have won in state and national competition; and number of students cited for excellence by national academic organizations.

Teacher experience. As previously stated, a balance of young and more experienced teachers is desirable. A median in the neighborhood of 15 years would indicate such a balance.

Teacher salaries. You want these three figures: salary for a beginning teacher with a bachelor's degree, top salary for a teacher with advance degrees and most experience, and an average salary.

Workbook

Now that you know most of the questions to ask, observations to make, and data to collect, it's time to get to work. The following pages are your workbook. Space is provided so that you can write in responses to questions, results of observations, and statistics for any three schools you are evaluating. The entries here are in the same order as they were in Sections 2, 3, and 4. If you expect to conduct more than three evaluations, you are welcome to photocopy the workbook pages. First, enter the name(s) of the school(s) you are evaluating.

School 1 _____

School 2 _____

School 3 _____

SECONDARY SCHOOL: QUESTIONS, ANSWERS, AND NOTES

WHAT ARE THE SCHOOL'S GOALS?

Notes:

School 1 _____

_____

_____

School 2 _____

_____

_____

School 3 _____

_____

_____

IS THE SCHOOL ENGAGED IN STRATEGIC PLANNING?

Answers: **School 1:** Yes/No   **School 2:** Yes/No   **School 3:** Yes/No

Notes:

School 1 _____

_____

_____

School 2 _____

_____

_____

School 3 _____

_____

_____

WHAT IS THE POLICY ON TRACKING AND PLACEMENT?

Notes:

School 1 _____

_____

_____

_____

School 2 _____

_____

_____

_____

School 3 _____

_____

_____

_____

WHAT IS THE POLICY ON ABILITY GROUPING?

Notes:

School 1 _____

_____

_____

_____

School 2 _____

_____

_____

_____

School 3 _____

_____

_____

_____

DOES THE SCHOOL PRACTICE SCHOOL-BASED MANAGEMENT?

Answers: **School 1:** Yes/No **School 2:** Yes/No **School 3:** Yes/No

Notes:

School 1 _____

_____

_____

School 2 _____

_____

_____

School 3 _____

_____

_____

WHAT IS THE ATTENDANCE POLICY?

Notes:

School 1 _____

_____

_____

_____

School 2 _____

_____

_____

_____

School 3 _____

_____

_____

_____

WHAT IS THE HOMEWORK POLICY?

Notes:

School 1 _____

_____

_____

_____

School 2 _____

_____

_____

_____

School 3 _____

_____

_____

_____

HOW MANY PRINCIPALS (HEADMASTERS) HAS THE SCHOOL HAD IN THE PAST 15 YEARS?

Answers: **School 1** _____   **School 2** _____   **School 3** _____

Notes:

School 1 _____

_____

_____

School 2 _____

_____

_____

School 3 _____

_____

_____

HOW MANY ADMINISTRATORS ARE THERE, AND WHAT ARE THEIR DUTIES?

Answers: **School 1** _____   **School 2** _____   **School 3** _____

Notes:

School 1 _____

_____

_____

_____

School 2 _____

_____

_____

_____

School 3 _____

_____

_____

_____

WHAT ARE THE REQUIREMENTS FOR ADMISSION?

Notes:

School 1 _____

_____

_____

School 2 _____

_____

_____

School 3 _____

_____

_____

WHAT KIND OF ORIENTATION IS OFFERED STUDENTS AND PARENTS?

Notes:

School 1 _____

_____

_____

_____

_____

School 2 _____

_____

_____

_____

_____

School 3 _____

_____

_____

_____

_____

WHAT SCHOLARSHIPS OR OTHER FINANCIAL AID IS AVAILABLE?

Notes:

School 1 _____

_____

_____

_____

School 2 _____

_____

_____

_____

School 3 _____

_____

_____

_____

**WHAT KNOWLEDGE AND SKILLS SHOULD A STUDENT IN SECONDARY
SCHOOL BE LEARNING?**

Notes:

School 1 _____

_____

_____

_____

School 2 _____

_____

_____

_____

School 3 _____

_____

_____

_____

HOW IS CURRICULUM DECIDED?

Notes:

School 1 _____

_____

_____

_____

School 2 _____

_____

_____

_____

School 3 _____

_____

_____

_____

WHAT ELECTIVES ARE OFFERED, AND IS CHOICE CONTROLLED?

Notes:

School 1 _____

_____

_____

_____

School 2 _____

_____

_____

_____

School 3 _____

_____

_____

_____

IS THE VOCATIONAL-TECHNICAL CURRICULUM CURRENT?

Answers: **School 1:** Yes/No **School 2:** Yes/No **School 3:** Yes/No

Notes:

School 1 _____

_____

_____

School 2 _____

_____

_____

School 3 _____

_____

_____

HOW OFTEN ARE CURRICULUM AND TEXTBOOKS REVIEWED?

Answers: **School 1** _____ **School 2** _____ **School 3** _____

Notes:

School 1 _____

_____

_____

_____

School 2 _____

_____

_____

_____

School 3 _____

_____

_____

_____

WHAT IS THE CURRICULUM IN THE ARTS?

Notes:

School 1 _____

_____

_____

_____

School 2 _____

_____

_____

_____

School 3 _____

_____

_____

_____

HOW ARE COMPUTERS USED FOR INSTRUCTION?

Notes:

School 1 _____

_____

_____

_____

School 2 _____

_____

_____

_____

School 3 _____

_____

_____

_____

IS THE LIBRARY WELL STOCKED AND WELL-EQUIPPED?

Answers: **School 1:** Yes/No   **School 2:** Yes/No   **School 3:** Yes/No

Notes:

School 1 _____

_____

_____

School 2 _____

_____

_____

School 3 _____

_____

_____

DOES THE CURRICULUM REFLECT MULTICULTURISM?

Answers: **School 1:** Yes/No   **School 2:** Yes/No   **School 3:** Yes/No

Notes:

School 1 _____

_____

_____

_____

School 2 _____

_____

_____

_____

School 3 _____

_____

_____

_____

IS THERE INTERDISCIPLINARY INSTRUCTION?

Answers: **School 1:** Yes/No   **School 2:** Yes/No   **School 3:** Yes/No

Notes:

School 1 _____

_____

_____

School 2 _____

_____

_____

School 3 _____

_____

_____

IS COURSE SCHEDULING FLEXIBLE?

Answers: **School 1:** Yes/No   **School 2:** Yes/No   **School 3:** Yes/No

Notes:

School 1 _____

_____

_____

_____

School 2 _____

_____

_____

_____

School 3 _____

_____

_____

_____

DOES THE HIGH SCHOOL OFFER ADVANCED PLACEMENT COURSES?

Answers: **School 1:** Yes/No   **School 2:** Yes/No   **School 3:** Yes/No

Notes:

School 1 _____

_____

School 2 _____

_____

School 3 _____

_____

WHAT IS THE SCHOOL'S DISCIPLINARY POLICY?

Notes:

School 1 _____

_____

_____

_____

_____

School 2 _____

_____

_____

_____

_____

School 3 _____

_____

_____

_____

_____

DOES THE SCHOOL HAVE AN EFFECTIVE POLICY FOR ONGOING MAINTENANCE AND REPAIR AND LONG-TERM RENOVATIONS?

Answers: **School 1:** Yes/No   **School 2:** Yes/No   **School 3:** Yes/No

Notes:

School 1 _____

_____

_____

School 2 _____

_____

_____

School 3 _____

_____

_____

HOW ACTIVE ARE THE PARENTS OF CHILDREN?

Notes:

School 1 _____

_____

_____

_____

School 2 _____

_____

_____

_____

School 3 _____

_____

_____

_____

HOW ACCESSIBLE TO PARENTS ARE THE TEACHERS?

Notes:

School 1 _____

_____

_____

_____

School 2 _____

_____

_____

_____

School 3 _____

_____

_____

_____

DOES THE SCHOOL'S GOVERNING BOARD AND ADMINISTRATION REGULARLY INFORM PARENTS AND THE COMMUNITY ABOUT SCHOOL POLICIES, PROGRAMS, AND ACTIVITIES?

Answers: **School 1:** Yes/No   **School 2:** Yes/No   **School 3:** Yes/No

Notes:

School 1 _____

_____

_____

School 2 _____

_____

_____

School 3 _____

_____

_____

CAN YOU OBSERVE CLASSES IN SESSION?

Answers: **School 1:** Yes/No   **School 2:** Yes/No   **School 3:** Yes/No

Notes:

School 1 _____

_____

_____

School 2 _____

_____

_____

School 3 _____

_____

_____

WHAT IS THE SCHOOL POLICY ON SECURITY?

Notes:

School 1 _____

_____

_____

_____

School 2 _____

_____

_____

_____

School 3 _____

_____

_____

_____

WHAT EXTRACURRICULAR ACTIVITIES ARE AVAILABLE TO STUDENTS?

Notes:

School 1 _____

_____

_____

_____

School 2 _____

_____

_____

_____

School 3 _____

_____

_____

_____

ARE VERY BRIGHT STUDENTS CHALLENGED?

Answers: **School 1:** Yes/No   **School 2:** Yes/No   **School 3:** Yes/No

Notes:

School 1 _____

_____

_____

School 2 _____

_____

_____

School 3 _____

_____

_____

IN A LARGE SCHOOL, WHAT HAS BEEN DONE TO PREVENT STUDENTS FROM BECOMING "LOST" IN THE CROWD?

Notes:

School 1 _____

_____

_____

_____

School 2 _____

_____

_____

_____

School 3 _____

_____

_____

_____

IS THERE BALANCE AMONG THE FACULTY?

Answers: **School 1:** Yes/No **School 2:** Yes/No **School 3:** Yes/No

Notes:

School 1 _____

_____

_____

School 2 _____

_____

_____

School 3 _____

_____

_____

DOES THE SCHOOL HAVE A STRONG, ONGOING TEACHER DEVELOPMENT PROGRAM?

Answers: **School 1:** Yes/No   **School 2:** Yes/No   **School 3:** Yes/No

Notes:

School 1 _____

_____

_____

School 2 _____

_____

_____

School 3 _____

_____

_____

ARE TEACHERS PREPARED AND ENCOURAGED TO PRACTICE DIFFERENT TEACHING STYLES AND LEARNING METHODS?

Answers: **School 1:** Yes/No   **School 2:** Yes/No   **School 3:** Yes/No

Notes:

School 1 _____

_____

_____

_____

School 2 _____

_____

_____

_____

School 3 _____

_____

_____

_____

DOES THE SCHOOL HAVE ENOUGH COUNSELORS AND OTHER SPECIALISTS?

Answers: **School 1:** Yes/No   **School 2:** Yes/No   **School 3:** Yes/No

Notes:

School 1 _____

_____

_____

School 2 _____

_____

_____

School 3 _____

_____

_____

ARE TEACHER AIDES USED?

Answers: **School 1:** Yes/No   **School 2:** Yes/No   **School 3:** Yes/No

Notes:

School 1 _____

_____

_____

_____

School 2 _____

_____

_____

_____

School 3 _____

_____

_____

_____

DOES THE SCHOOL PRACTICE AUTHENTIC ASSESSMENT?

Answers: **School 1:** Yes/No   **School 2:** Yes/No   **School 3:** Yes/No

Notes:

School 1 _____

_____

_____

School 2 _____

_____

_____

School 3 _____

_____

_____

HOW DO TEACHERS USE TEST RESULTS?

Notes:

School 1 _____

_____

_____

_____

School 2 _____

_____

_____

_____

School 3 _____

_____

_____

_____

HOW ARE TEST RESULTS REPORTED TO STUDENTS AND PARENTS?

Notes:

School 1 _____

_____

_____

_____

School 2 _____

_____

_____

_____

School 3 _____

_____

_____

_____

WHAT IS THE TRANSPORTATION POLICY?

Notes:

School 1 _____

_____

_____

_____

School 2 _____

_____

_____

_____

School 3 _____

_____

_____

_____

ARE STUDENTS ACTIVELY ENGAGED IN LEARNING?

Answers: **School 1:** Yes/No   **School 2:** Yes/No   **School 3:** Yes/No

Notes:

School 1 _____

_____

_____

_____

School 2 _____

_____

_____

_____

School 3 _____

_____

_____

_____

ARE STUDENTS ROAMING THE HALLS DURING CLASSES?

Answers: **School 1:** Yes/No   **School 2:** Yes/No   **School 3:** Yes/No

Notes:

School 1 _____

_____

_____

School 2 _____

_____

_____

School 3 _____

_____

_____

ARE STUDENTS' WORK AND AWARDS DISPLAYED PROMINENTLY?

Answers: **School 1:** Yes/No   **School 2:** Yes/No   **School 3:** Yes/No

Notes:

School 1 _____

_____

_____

School 2 _____

_____

_____

School 3 _____

_____

_____

IS THE SCHOOL CLEAN AND WELL MAINTAINED?

Answers: **School 1:** Yes/No   **School 2:** Yes/No   **School 3:** Yes/No

Notes:

School 1 _____

_____

_____

_____

School 2 _____

_____

_____

_____

School 3 _____

_____

_____

_____

IS THE SCHOOL SECURE FROM UNAUTHORIZED VISITORS?

Answers: **School 1:** Yes/No   **School 2:** Yes/No   **School 3:** Yes/No

Notes:

School 1 _____

_____

_____

_____

School 2 _____

_____

_____

_____

School 3 _____

_____

_____

_____

ARE THERE ADEQUATE AND UP-TO-DATE MATERIALS AND EQUIPMENT?

Answers: **School 1:** Yes/No   **School 2:** Yes/No   **School 3:** Yes/No

Notes:

School 1 _____

_____

_____

School 2 _____

_____

_____

School 3 _____

_____

_____

AVERAGE DAILY ATTENDANCE (ADA)

Answers: **School 1** _____   **School 2** _____   **School 3** _____

Notes:

School 1 _____

_____

_____

School 2 _____

_____

_____

School 3 _____

_____

_____

CLASSROOM TEACHER:STUDENT RATIO

Answers: **School 1** ____ : ____   **School 2** ____ : ____   **School 3** ____ : ____

Notes:

School 1 _____

_____

_____

_____

School 2 _____

_____

_____

_____

School 3 _____

_____

_____

COMPETENCY TEST PERFORMANCE (OVER 5 YEARS)

Answers (percentage passing by grade 12):

School 1:

Reading: Year ____ % ____   Year ____ % ____   Year ____ % ____
Year ____ % ____   Year ____ % ____

Writing: Year ____ % ____   Year ____ % ____   Year ____ % ____
Year ____ % ____   Year ____ % ____

Math: Year ____ % ____   Year ____ % ____   Year ____ % ____
Year ____ % ____   Year ____ % ____

School 2:

Reading: Year ____ % ____   Year ____ % ____   Year ____ % ____
Year ____ % ____   Year ____ % ____

Writing: Year ____ % ____   Year ____ % ____   Year ____ % ____
Year ____ % ____   Year ____ % ____

Math: Year ____ % ____   Year ____ % ____   Year ____ % ____
Year ____ % ____   Year ____ % ____

School 3:

Reading: Year ____ % ____   Year ____ % ____   Year ____ % ____
Year ____ % ____   Year ____ % ____

Writing: Year ____ % ____   Year ____ % ____   Year ____ % ____
Year ____ % ____   Year ____ % ____

Math: Year ____ % ____   Year ____ % ____   Year ____ % ____
Year ____ % ____   Year ____ % ____

Notes:

School 1 _____

_____

_____

_____

_____

School 2 _____

_____

_____

_____

_____

School 3 _____

_____

_____

_____

_____

COUNSELOR:STUDENT RATIO

Answers: **School 1** ___ : ___   **School 2** ___ : ___   **School 3** ___ : ___

Notes:

School 1 _____

_____

_____

_____

_____

School 2 _____

_____

_____

_____

_____

School 3 _____

_____

_____

_____

_____

CURRENT EXPENDITURE PER PUPIL (OVER 5 YEARS)

Answers:

School 1: Year ____ $ ____   Year ____ $ ____   Year ____ $ ____
         Year ____ $ ____   Year ____ $ ____

School 2: Year ____ $ ____   Year ____ $ ____   Year ____ $ ____
         Year ____ $ ____   Year ____ $ ____

School 3: Year ____ $ ____   Year ____ $ ____   Year ____ $ ____
         Year ____ $ ____   Year ____ $ ____

Notes:

School 1 _____

_____

_____

_____

_____

_____

School 2 _____

_____

_____

_____

_____

_____

School 3 _____

_____

_____

_____

_____

_____

DROPOUT RATE (OVER 5 YEARS)

Answers:

School 1: Year _____ % _____   Year _____ % _____   Year _____ % _____
              Year _____ % _____   Year _____ % _____

School 2: Year _____ % _____   Year _____ % _____   Year _____ % _____
              Year _____ % _____   Year _____ % _____

School 3: Year _____ % _____   Year _____ % _____   Year _____ % _____
              Year _____ % _____   Year _____ % _____

Notes:

School 1 _____
          _____
          _____
          _____
          _____
          _____

School 2 _____
          _____
          _____
          _____
          _____
          _____

School 3 _____
          _____
          _____
          _____
          _____
          _____

GRADUATION RATE (OVER 5 YEARS)

Answers:

School 1: Year ____ % ____   Year ____ % ____   Year ____ % ____

Year ____ % ____   Year ____ % ____

School 2: Year ____ % ____   Year ____ % ____   Year ____ % ____

Year ____ % ____   Year ____ % ____

School 3: Year ____ % ____   Year ____ % ____   Year ____ % ____

Year ____ % ____   Year ____ % ____

Notes:

School 1 _____

_____

_____

_____

_____

_____

School 2 _____

_____

_____

_____

_____

_____

School 3 _____

_____

_____

_____

_____

_____

PERCENTAGE OF GRADUATES WHO GO ON TO HIGHER EDUCATION

Answers: **School 1 _____%**   **School 2 _____%**   **School 3 _____%**

Notes:

School 1 _____

_____

_____

School 2 _____

_____

_____

School 3 _____

_____

_____

STUDENTS PER COMPUTER USED FOR INSTRUCTION

Answers: **School 1 ___ : ___**   **School 2 ___ : ___**   **School 3 ___ : ___**

Notes:

School 1 _____

_____

_____

_____

School 2 _____

_____

_____

_____

School 3 _____

_____

_____

_____

PERCENTAGE OF STUDENTS TAKING SAT OR ACT (OVER 5 YEARS)

Answers:

School 1: Year ____ % ____   Year ____ % ____   Year ____ % ____
            Year ____ % ____   Year ____ % ____

School 2: Year ____ % ____   Year ____ % ____   Year ____ % ____
            Year ____ % ____   Year ____ % ____

School 3: Year ____ % ____   Year ____ % ____   Year ____ % ____
            Year ____ % ____   Year ____ % ____

Notes:

School 1 _____

_____

_____

_____

_____

_____

School 2 _____

_____

_____

_____

_____

_____

School 3 _____

_____

_____

_____

_____

_____

AVERAGE COMBINED SCORE ON SAT OR ACT (OVER 5 YEARS)

Answers:

School 1: Year ____ / ____   Year ____ / ____   Year ____ / ____

             Year ____ / ____   Year ____ / ____

School 2: Year ____ / ____   Year ____ / ____   Year ____ / ____

             Year ____ / ____   Year ____ / ____

School 3: Year ____ / ____   Year ____ / ____   Year ____ / ____

             Year ____ / ____   Year ____ / ____

Notes:

School 1 _____

_____

School 2 _____

_____

School 3 _____

_____

STUDENTS ENROLLED IN AP COURSES, AND NUMBER OF AP COURSES

Answers: **School 1** ____ : ____   **School 2** ____ : ____   **School 3** ____ : ____

Notes:

School 1 _____

_____

_____

School 2 _____

_____

_____

School 3 _____

_____

_____

STUDENTS EARNING AWARDS AND HONORS

Answers: **School 1** _____ **School 2** _____ **School 3** _____

Notes:

School 1 _____

_____

_____

_____

School 2 _____

_____

_____

_____

School 3 _____

_____

_____

_____

MEDIAN YEARS OF TEACHER EXPERIENCE

Answers: **School 1** _____ **School 2** _____ **School 3** _____

Notes:

School 1 _____

_____

_____

School 2 _____

_____

_____

School 3 _____

_____

_____

TEACHER SALARY FIGURES

Answers:

Beginning salary:	**School 1** $_____	**School 2** $_____	**School 3** $_____
Top salary:	**School 1** $_____	**School 2** $_____	**School 3** $_____
Avg. Salary:	**School 1** $_____	**School 2** $_____	**School 3** $_____

Notes:

School 1 _____

_____

_____

_____

School 2 _____

_____

_____

_____

School 3 _____

_____

_____

_____

APPENDIX A

People Resources

I am grateful to a number of people for their invaluable information and guidance. Two people were particularly helpful in the beginning by assisting me in developing the questions to ask, observations to make, and data to collect. For Part 3, Evaluating an Elementary School, I am indebted to Ronald J. Areglado, associate executive director of programs for the National Association of Elementary School Principals. Helping me with Part 4, Evaluating a Secondary School, was John A. Lammel, director of high school services for the National Association of Secondary School Principals.

In addition to offering guidance at the start, these two men were kind enough to read the manuscript draft and suggest changes and corrections.

Ron Areglado and June Million, director of public information for NAESP, worked with me in the preparation of the questionnaire that was mailed by NAESP to approximately 3,500 of its members in January and February 1994. Twenty percent of the questionnaires, or about 700, were completed and returned by elementary school principals from all parts of the country and from urban, suburban, and rural schools.

The survey was titled "What Should Parents Ask About and Look for When Choosing a School?" The principals were asked to choose from among 31 "questions parents should ask" the ones they considered to be most important, important, and least important.

Based on the principals' choices, we compiled a list of the 10 most important questions parents should ask about a school they are evaluating. These are the 10 questions, listed in the order of their ranking by the principals:

1. What is the classroom:student ratio?
2. Does the school have a well-equipped and well-used library/media center?

3. Does the reading program balance whole language and phonics?
4. How are computers used for instruction?
5. What is the school's disciplinary policy?
6. What is the teaching philosophy (i.e., lecturing, group and individual instruction, teams)?
7. Are there professional specialists to support the school program?
8. How is student progress (grades) reported?
9. How often are textbooks reviewed?
10. Can parents meet with teachers other than during traditional school hours?

The principals also were asked to rank a list of 10 "important things for parents to look for."

The five most critical observations, according to the principals, are as follows:

1. Do students appear to be actively involved in learning?
2. Do teachers appear to manage classroom discipline effectively?
3. Is students' work prominently displayed in classrooms and hallways?
4. Are parents/others warmly welcomed as visitors?
5. Is the school clean and in good repair inside and out?

Other people whom I interviewed while researching for the book and who provided wise counsel are as follows:

Peter Bachmann, headmaster, Flintridge Preparatory School, La Canada, CA.

Chrissie Bamber, director, the National Committee for Citizens in Education.

Patte Barth, editor of Basic Education, the monthly publication of the Council for Basic Education.

Ron Ganschinietz, principal, Collinsville High School, Collinsville, IL.

Robert A. Hochstein, assistant to the president of the Carnegie Foundation for the Advancement of Teaching.

Donna Harrison, first-grade teacher, Franklinville, NJ.

Amy Hoffman, parent, Citizens Alliance for Educational Excellence, Matarie, LA.

Patricia Lucas, principal, Manatee High School, Bradenton, FL.

Nancy McFarland, parent, Citizens for Positive Education, Coshocton, OH.

Catherine O'Neill, editor of Independent School, the magazine of the National Association of Independent Schools.

Jeanne D. Parker, assistant to the superintendent, Montclair, NJ, Public School District.

Paula Stein, parent, Montclair, NJ.

Valerie Sweatt, parent, Montclair, NJ.

Lois Tigay, parent, Montclair, NJ.

Lincoln Turner, parent, Montclair, NJ.

Ruth Wattenberg, deputy director, Educational Issues Department, American Federation of Teachers.

MATERIAL RESOURCES: BIBLIOGRAPHY

American Library Association. *Educational Excellence Through Effective School Library Media Programs.* Chicago: American Library Association, 1989.

Barth, Patte, and Ruth Mitchell. *Smart Start.* Golden, CO: North American Press, 1992.

Berla, Nancy, Anne T. Henderson, and William Kerewsky. *The Middle School Years.* Washington, DC: National Committee for Citizens in Education, 1991.

Boyer, Ernest L. *High School.* New York: Harper & Row, 1983.

_____. *Ready to Learn.* Princeton, NJ: The Carnegie Foundation for the Advancement of Teaching, 1991.

College Board (The). *Academic Preparation for College.* New York: The College Board, 1983

Goodlad, John I. *A Place Called School.* New York: McGraw-Hill Book Company, 1983.

Grant, Gerald. *The World We Created at Hamilton High.* Cambridge, MA: Harvard University Press, 1988.

Murphy, John, and Jeffry Schiller. *Transforming America's Schools*. La Salle, IL: Open Court Publishing Company, 1992.

National Association of Independent Schools. *Parent's Guide*. Washington, DC: National Association of Independent Schools, 1993.

National Committee for Citizens in Education (The). *Parent Rights Card*. Washington, DC: The National Committee for Citizens in Education, 1992.

Neal, Richard G. *School Based Management*. Bloomington, IN: National Educational Service, 1991.

Pellicer, Leonard O., et al. *High School Leaders and Their Schools*. Reston, VA: National Association of Secondary School Principals, 1988.

Rioux, William. *You Can Improve Your Child's School*. New York: Simon & Schuster, 1980.

Thomas, M. Donald. *Your School: How Well Is It Working?* Washington, DC: The National Committee for Citizens in Education, 1982.

U.S. Department of Education. *Choosing a School for Your Child*. Washington, DC: U.S. Department of Education, 1989.

APPENDIX B

Comparative Data and References: What Students Should Know

In recent years, teams of scholars have been developing national standards in a number of subjects. Most of these standards will be in place by 1995–96. More and more, they will guide curriculum and testing in America's public schools. If you are evaluating a public school, we suggest you contact the appropriate state department of education to ask about the use of national standards. A listing of state education departments is included in this appendix.

Some guidance as to what students at various grade levels should be learning is offered by the frameworks and objectives adopted for the National Assessment of Educational Progress (NAEP). For more than 20 years, the federal government has asked NAEP to assess what America's children are learning at the elementary, middle, and high school levels (grades 4, 8, and 12). We thought it might be helpful to know what the educators who developed the NAEP survey consider vital learning objectives for students.

In reading, the scholars have identified three reading purposes: (1) reading for literary experience, (2) reading to be informed, and (3) reading to perform a task. At the fourth grade, 55 percent of the items on the NAEP reading survey are devoted to reading for literary experience; only 40 percent and 35 percent, respectively, at the eighth and twelfth grades. The breakdown for the other two purposes is as follows: reading to be informed: 45, 40, and 45 percent; reading to perform a task: 0, 20, and 20 percent.

Naturally, the reading samples and questions vary for the three age groups, but here are typical questions posed to determine students' initial understanding, interpretation, personal reflection/response, and critical evaluation:

Reading for literary experience: What is the story/plot about? How did the plot develop? How would you describe the main character? How did this character change from the beginning to the end of the story? How did this character change your idea of _____ ? Is this story similar to or different from your own experience? Rewrite the story with _____ as a setting or _____ as a character. How does this author's use of _____ (irony, personification, humor) contribute to _____ ?

Reading for information: What does this article tell you about _____ ? What does the author think about this topic? What caused this event? In what ways are these ideas important to the topic or theme? What current event does this remind you of? Does this description fit what you know about _____? Why? How useful would this article be for _____ ? Explain. What could be added to improve the author's argument?

Reading to perform a task: What is this supposed to help you do? What time can you get a nonstop flight to _____ ? What will be the result of this step in the directions? What must you do before this step? In order to _____ , what information would you need to find that you don't know right now? Describe a situation where you could leave out step _____ ? Why is this information needed? What would happen if you omitted this?

The NAEP mathematics survey tests three abilities: conceptual understanding, procedural knowledge, and problem solving. Under these categories are included numbers and operations; measurement; geometry; data analysis, statistics, and probability; algebra and functions.

Here are some of the skills NAEP expects students to have mastered at the three grade levels:

Numbers and operations: Students at grade 4 should be able to add subtract, multiply, and divide whole numbers, simple fractions, and decimals. At grade 8, students should be able to work with signed numbers and numbers expressed in scientific notation. Also, they should be able to work with elementary powers and roots. Students in grade 12 are expected to have a much greater understanding in these areas.

Measurement: Grade-4 students should have a basic knowledge of length, area, capacity, weight, mass, angle, time, money, and temperature. At the higher grades, students are expected to have a greater grasp of these skills.

Geometry: Geometry skills are mostly learned in grades 8 and 12. Students in those grades are expected to recognize and model geometric figures in one, two, and three dimensions. Also, they should be able to understand and express geometric relationships.

Data analysis, statistics, and probability: Fourth-graders should be able to read and interpret simple tables and graphs and determine the probability of simple events (the odds of something happening). Older students should know about selecting an unbiased sample in data collection, recognizing the use and misuse of statistics, charting data on a graph or chart, and describing more sophisticated statistical relationships.

Algebra and functions: Students in grade 8 should have some basic familiarity with algebraic equations, but students in grade 12 should have mastered higher-level skills, including the ability to apply the concepts of trigonometry.

In Part 4 (Secondary School), we referred to the College Board booklet *Academic Preparation for College.* This booklet can tell you what knowledge and skills your child needs to have for the best chance of success in college. Single copies of the booklet are available at no cost from the Office of Academic Affairs, the College Board, 45 Columbus Avenue, New York, NY 10023-6992. If you belong to a parents' group, the booklet can be ordered in quantities of 20, at a cost of $20, from the Publications Office of the College Board.

SELECTED STATISTICS

The National Education Association annually publishes *Estimates of [Public] School Statistics.* The combined elementary/secondary statistics listed on the next page are estimates for the school year 1993–94 based on data supplied by state education departments.

State	Average daily * attendance, %	Average teacher salary, $	Current expenditure per pupil in ADA, $
New England			
CT	95	49,500	8,429
ME	95	30,996	6,046
MA	94	39,370	6,612
NH	95	36,372	5,994
RI	94	39,261	6,764
VT	93	36,043	7,721
Mideast			
DE	93	37,469	6,587
DC	90	42,543	8,632
MD	93	39,937	6,502
NJ	94	45,308	10,062
NY	92	46,800	8,601
PA	93	43,688	8,220
Southeast			
AL	95	28,705	4,061
AR	95	27,873	3,949
FL	93	32,020	5,336
GA	94	30,456	4,473
KY	95	31,582	5,174
LA	93	28,508	4,807
MS	96	25,235	3,430
NC	95	29,680	4,972
SC	97	30,190	4,546
TN	94	30,037	4,199
VA	94	33,128	5,556
WV	93	30,549	5,790
Great Lakes			
IL	93	40,989	5,520
IN	96	36,255	5,890
MI	NA	42,500	6,574
OH	92	35,700	6,270
WI	94	36,644	7,001

State	Average daily * attendance, %	Average teacher salary, $	Current expenditure per pupil in ADA, $
Plains			
IA	94	30,760	5,634
KS	96	34,178	5,653
MN	94	36,146	5,770
MO	NA	30,227	4,642
NE	95	29,564	5,194
ND	96	25,508	4,449
SD	96	25,199	4,733
Southwest			
AZ	94	31,680	4,286
NM	90	27,922	4,966
OK	94	26,749	4,162
TX	NA	30,519	5,069
Rocky Mountains			
CO	NA	33,826	4,584
ID	NA	27,803	4,208
MT	95	28,210	5,276
UT	94	28,056	3,419
WY	95	30,310	5,924
Far West			
AK	87	46,581	9,811
CA	NA	40,289	4,621
HI	94	36,564	5,936
NV	93	33,955	4,959
OR	93	37,130	6,068
WA	94	35,860	5,759

* Percentage of the average number of students enrolled in elementary and secondary schools on a daily basis who actually attended school. The difference between these figures and 100% is an indication of average daily absence. The figures have been rounded off (e.g., 95.8% becomes 96%, and 94.1% becomes 94%).

The U.S. Department of Education has reported an overall decrease of almost 4 percent in the nation's dropout rate from 1972 to 1992. The rate is figured this way: the percentage of persons aged 16 to 24 who are not enrolled in school and have not graduated from high school or received an equivalency certificate. The Department reported a dropout rate of 14.6 percent in 1972 and an 11-percent rate in 1992. However, the questionnaire used to determine dropout data was changed in 1992, so the 1992 figure might be slightly higher if computed according to the method used in previous years.

STATE EDUCATION DEPARTMENTS

This listing includes the address for each state education department and the phone number for the office of the state superintendent or commissioner. When writing, begin: State Department of Education, followed by the address given below.

Alabama: Gordon Persons Office, 50 N Ripley St, Montgomery, AL 36130-3901; (205) 242-9700.

Alaska: 801 W 10th St, Suite 200, Juneau, AK 99801-1894; (907) 465-2800.

Arizona: 1535 W Jefferson, Phoenix, AZ 85007; (602) 542-5156.

Arkansas: 4 State Capitol Mall, Little Rock, AR 72201-1071; (501) 682-4204.

California: PO Box 944272, 721 Capitol Mall, Sacramento, CA 94244-2720; (916) 657-5485.

Colorado: 201 E Colfax Ave, Denver, CO 80203-1705; (303) 866-6806.

Connecticut: PO Box 2219, 165 Capitol Ave, Hartford, CT 06145; (203) 566-5061.

Delaware: PO Box 1402 Townsend Bldg, Dover, DE 19903; (302) 739-4601.

District of Columbia: Presidential Bldg, 415 12th St, NW, Washington, DC 20004; (202) 724-4222.

Florida: Capitol Bldg, PL-08, Talahassee, FL 32399-0400; (904) 487-1785.

Georgia: 2066 Twin Towers East, 205 Butler St, Atlanta, GA 30334; (404) 656-2800.

Hawaii: PO Box 2360, Honolulu, HI 96804; (808) 586-3230.

Idaho: Jordan Office Bldg, 650 W State St, Boise, ID 83720; (208) 334-3300.

Illinois: 100 N First St, Springfield, IL 62777; (217) 782-2221.

Indiana: Rm 229, State House, 100 N Capitol St, Indianapolis, IN 46204-2798; (317) 232-6665.

Iowa: Grimes State Office Bldg, Des Moines, IA 50319-0146; (515) 281-5294.

Kansas: 120 E Tenth St, Topeka, KS 66612; (913) 296-3202.

Kentucky: Capitol Plaza Tower, 500 Mero St, Frankfort, KY 40601; (502) 564-3141.

Louisiana: PO Box 94064, Baton Rouge, LA 70804-9064; (504) 342-3602.

Maine: State House, Station #23, Augusta, ME 04333; (207) 287-5800.

Maryland: 200 W Baltimore St, Baltimore, MD 21201; (410) 333-2200.

Massachusetts: 350 Main St, Malden, MA 02148-5023; (617) 388-3300.

Michigan: PO Box 30008, Lansing, MI 48909; (517) 373-3354.

Minnesota: 712 Capitol Square Bldg, 550 Cedar St, St Paul, MN 55101; (612) 296-2358.

Mississippi: PO Box 771, Jackson, MS 39205-0771; (601) 359-3513.

Missouri: PO 480, Jefferson City, MO 65102; (314) 751-4446.

Montana: 106 State Capitol, Helena, MT 59620; (406) 444-3680.

Nebraska: 301 Centennial Mall South, PO Box 94987, Lincoln, NE 68509; (402) 471-2465.

Nevada: Capitol Complex, 400 W King St, Carson City, NV 89710; (702) 687-3100.

New Hampshire: 101 Pleasant St, State Office Park South, Concord, NH 03301; (603) 271-3144.

New Jersey: 225 W State St, CN-500, Trenton, NJ 08625-0500; (609) 292-4450.

New Mexico: Education Bldg, 300 Don Gaspar, Santa Fe, NM 87501-2786; (505) 827-6516.

New York: 111 Education Bldg, Washington Ave, Albany, NY 12234; (518) 474-5844.

North Carolina: Education Bldg, 301 N Wilmington St, Raleigh, NC 27601-2825; (919) 715-1299.

North Dakota: 600 E Blvd Ave, Bismark, ND 58505-0164; (701) 224-2261.

Ohio: 65 S Front St, Columbus, OH 43266-0308; (614) 466-3304.

Oklahoma: 2500 N Lincoln Blvd, Oklahoma City, OK 73105-4599; (405) 521-3301.

Oregon: 700 Pringle Prky, SE, Salem, OR 97310; (503) 378-3573.

Pennsylvania: 333 Market St, Harrisburg, PA 17126-0333; (717) 787-5829.

Rhode Island: 22 Hayes St, Providence, RI 02908; (401) 277-2031.

South Carolina: Rutledge Bldg, 1429 Senate St, Columbia, SC 29201; (803) 734-8492.

South Dakota: 700 Governors Dr, Pierre, SD 57501; (605) 773-3134.

Tennessee: 100 Cordell Hull Bldg, Nashville, TN 37243-0375; (615) 741-2731.

Texas: 1701 N Congress Ave, Austin, TX 78701-1494; (512) 463-8985.

Utah: 250 E 500 South, Salt Lake City, UT 84111; (801) 538-7510.

Vermont: 120 State St, Montpelier, VT 05602-2703; (802) 828-3135.

Virginia: PO Box 6-Q, 101 N 14th St, Richmond, VA 23216-2060; (804) 225-2755.

Washington: Old Capitol Bldg, Legion & Franklin, PO Box 47200, Olympia, WA 98504-7200; (206) 586-6904.

West Virginia: 1900 Kanawha Blvd East, Charleston, WV 25305; (304) 558-2681.

Wisconsin: 125 S Webster St, PO Box 7841, Madison, WI 53707; (608) 266-1771.

Wyoming: Hathaway Bldg, 2300 Capitol Ave, Cheyenne, WY 82002; (307) 777-7675.

APPENDIX C
SAT© Averages by State

SAT® Averages by State 1984, 1991–1994

Comparing or ranking states on the basis of SAT scores alone
is invalid and strongly discouraged by the College Board

	1984		1991		1992		1993		1994		% Graduates Taking SAT*
	V	M	V	M	V	M	V	M	V	M	
Alabama	467	503	476	515	476	520	480	526	482	529	8
Alaska	443	471	439	481	433	475	438	477	434	477	49
Arizona	469	509	442	490	440	493	444	497	443	496	26
California	421	476	415	482	416	484	415	484	413	482	46
Colorado	468	514	453	506	453	507	454	509	456	513	28
Connecticut	436	468	429	468	430	470	430	474	426	472	80
Delaware	433	469	428	464	432	463	429	465	428	464	68
Dist. of Columbia	397	426	405	435	405	427	405	441	406	443	53
Florida	423	467	416	466	416	468	416	466	413	466	49
Georgia	392	430	400	444	398	444	399	445	398	446	65
Hawaii	395	474	405	478	401	477	401	478	401	480	58
Idaho	480	512	463	505	460	503	465	507	461	508	16
Illinois	463	518	471	535	473	537	475	541	478	546	14
Indiana	410	454	408	457	409	459	409	460	410	466	60
Iowa	519	570	515	578	512	584	520	583	506	574	5
Kansas	502	549	493	546	487	546	494	548	494	550	10
Kentucky	479	518	473	520	470	518	476	522	474	523	11
Louisiana	472	508	476	518	471	520	481	527	481	530	9
Maine	429	463	421	458	422	460	422	463	420	463	68
Maryland	429	468	429	475	431	476	431	478	429	479	64
Massachusetts	429	467	426	470	428	474	427	476	426	475	79
Michigan	461	515	461	519	464	523	469	528	472	537	11
Minnesota	481	539	480	543	492	561	489	556	495	562	9
Mississippi	480	512	477	520	478	526	481	521	485	528	4
Missouri	469	512	476	526	475	529	481	532	485	537	10
Montana	490	544	464	518	465	523	459	516	463	523	21
Nebraska	493	548	481	543	478	540	479	544	482	543	9
Nevada	442	489	435	484	434	488	432	488	429	484	30

	1984		1991		1992		1993		1994		% Graduates Taking SAT*
	V	M	V	M	V	M	V	M	V	M	
New Hampshire	448	483	440	481	440	483	442	487	438	486	69
New Jersey	418	458	417	469	420	471	419	473	418	475	71
New Mexico	487	527	474	522	475	521	478	525	475	528	12
New York	424	470	413	468	416	466	416	471	416	472	76
North Carolina	395	432	400	444	405	450	406	453	405	455	60
North Dakota	500	554	502	571	501	567	518	583	497	559	5
Ohio	460	508	450	496	450	501	454	505	456	510	24
Oklahoma	484	525	476	521	480	527	482	530	482	537	9
Oregon	435	472	439	483	439	486	441	492	436	491	53
Pennsylvania	425	462	417	459	418	459	418	460	417	462	70
Rhode Island	424	461	421	459	421	460	419	464	420	462	68
South Carolina	384	419	395	437	394	437	396	442	395	443	60
South Dakota	520	566	496	551	490	550	502	558	483	548	5
Tennessee	486	523	487	528	484	529	486	531	488	535	12
Texas	413	453	411	463	410	466	413	472	412	474	48
Utah	503	542	494	537	496	545	500	549	509	558	4
Vermont	437	470	424	466	429	468	426	467	427	472	68
Virginia	428	466	424	466	425	429	425	468	424	469	65
Washington	463	505	433	480	432	484	435	486	434	488	49
West Virginia	466	510	441	485	440	484	439	485	439	482	17
Wisconsin	475	532	481	542	481	548	485	551	487	557	9
Wyoming	489	545	466	514	462	516	463	507	459	521	12
National	*426*	*471*	*422*	*474*	*423*	*476*	*424*	*478*	*423*	*479*	*42*

* Based on number of high school graduates in 1994 as projected by the Western Interstate Commission for Higher Education, and number of students in the Class 1994 who took the SAT.

Note: If only a small percentage of students took the SAT, the average score is apt to be higher than if a greater number of students took the test. If the percentage of students taking the test and their average score are both high, a strong college-preparatory program is indicated. This is especially true at the district and school levels.

INDEX